FIVE OF US

BY LEN JENKIN

DRAMATISTS
PLAY SERVICE
INC.

FIVE OF US
Copyright © 1986, Len Jenkin

FIVE OF US was presented at La Mama E.T.C., in New York City, on February 13, 1984. It was directed by Lawrence Sacharow; the costume design was by Marianne Powell-Parker; the lighting design was Blu; and the stage manager was Rikki Grossberg. The cast was as follows:

HERMAN..Tom Noonan
MARK...David Strathairn
LEE..Polly Draper
CRYSTAL...Karen Young
EDDIE...Christopher McCann

CAST, in order of appearance:

HERMAN
MARK
LEE
CRYSTAL
EDDIE

The play takes place in New York City.

The time is now, from one afternoon to the following morning.

The directions in China traditionally number not four but five: North, South, East, West, and Center.

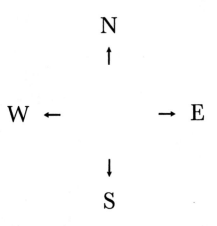

FIVE OF US

ACT I

Dim light. Herman the messenger, a man neither old nor young, is crossing the stage. He wears a ragged overcoat, a worn suit and tie, and has a package under one arm. He has a cassette tape recorder slung over one shoulder. Herman flips on his tape: late fifties rock and roll, a doo-wop number.
Herman hesitantly begins to dance, clumsily . . . and sing along, badly.
Lights come up, hard and bright. Street noise. Herman looks out at the audience, clicks off his tape recorder.

HERMAN. I am a messenger. I deliver. I work for the Pony Express Messenger Service. I have a bad back and my feet smell all the time.

I am very nice. I give everyone the feeling that they're better than me, and I'm scared of them, and they can order me around if they wish it. Even little kids. This talent for being weak and from the world of service often results in bad treatment and pain. Many people feel low themselves, so that when they get a chance to hurt a man they will do it. But to act this way is my nature, so that I have no choice but to be insulted, and often punched as well. However, some people, mostly ladies, are good to me because of this same feeling they get, and will give me coffee when I deliver, and tip. This I admire, as kindness in women is a fine thing and not to be despised, especially if there is not beauty.

I did not learn this way of being from my parents, who I do not know, but elsewhere. Where I cannot tell. I am a hard worker, and know where I learned this. There was a man named Berthold in the place I lived when I was small. His occupation was that of carpenter. "What is the way to do?" he would say in a foreign voice. And then he would forget where he was. The shavings curled onto the floor. Sweet smell. He made things. His wife was a terrible woman who kept their money in a tin box. She wanted to be strong and powerful with money like the

Director. This Berthold did not understand. She would scream at him to make him know what she wanted. But he could not help her.

Now I am a messenger, and that is not a carpenter. I make nothing. I take things from one place to another place, and even if you are only half-wise you will think it makes no difference to Sweet Jesus or the devil if these things are in one place or another place. You are pushing things around to nowhere, and your feet hurt. You will go and get something better, especially as it is not a living wage for people who have not very simple tastes.

My fellow workers are black children. Beneath their meanness and love of loud noises, some are intelligent. But they do not work hard, and have no loyalty, as they do not plan to spend their lives in the service. I know, as I have asked them. However, I must be a messenger and be happy, as on being hired by the Pony Express Messenger Service, I reached my peak of possible employment in this world, which does not suffer fools gladly but hospitalizes them, and I cannot take injections because of my falling weakness and trouble, so I have reached my apex of professionalization and must make the best of it. Which reminds me of my medicine. (*Herman looks at his watch, nods. He takes a vial of pills out of his pocket, and swallows one.*)

So, I have spent years in this service and the Pony Express gets love and loyalty from me, for without employment I would be in a room with a slot in the door for the tray. My boss, Mr. Ginetti, told me this. But they do not treat me with love and lovingness in return, but often yell and call me names. That is why I am filling my coffee cans, and now one can is full of paper money, and some silver. When all cans fill, I will visit mountains, and valleys, and the cities of the plain. (*He looks at his watch.*)

The little hand is on the five. This particular delivery has to wait . . . till tomorrow. As I am a person of certain habits, every day after working I go directly to the Diamond Topless Lounge where I drink beer and admiringly view the dancings. However, as I must protect this interesting package, and there are certain men at the Diamond Topless who sometimes make me give them money—today I am going directly home. (*Herman takes a few steps, stops.*)

In my home I do sleeping, and make reservations, and read

8

the Bible. This I do as I have the Bible, and many other books I do not have, excepting National Geographics, and another kind of book which I purchase often. My most recent purchase has the attractive title of "Lust in Bangkok." Its author is Abner Dewitt, which I believe to be a pseudo-anonymous alias of the true writer, who is my favorite. But it is my sexual life I refer to here, which is unsuitable for you, not as it is sexual of course — we are all modern — but because of the lonely and mental nature of my sexual doings which is not good I think for you to learn. So that is all about "Lust in Bangkok." The Bible, however, has taught me much, especially about the faithful servant, and I decided that is who I was . . . until today. (*Herman winks, tucks the package firmly under his arm, begins to walk off. He again flips on his cassette recorder. The same doo-wop number. Herman dances a bit, and exits. Lights and sound fade.*)

Lights up on a room in a tenement apartment. Bookcases made of orange crates, old couch, posters, a refrigerator and a kitchen sink. There are some anthropological artifacts, none of any value: an Indonesian ritual mask, Hopi Kachina dolls. There is a door into a bathroom, and another, the front door, leading out into the building's hallway. There's a window in the rear wall, facing the street. Late afternoon light outside. There are two suitcases near the door.

Mark, early thirties, sits on a rolling stool at a long desk made out of a door. There are three typewriters spaced out along the desk in a line. The typewriters have rolls of paper running through them, the three rollers mounted on the wall behind. The paper to be typed on is thus continuous, and long sections of it have already been typed on all three machines, and curl over onto the floor.

Mark looks at the writing on typewriter one, then on typewriter two, then three. He lights a cigarette, paces the room. He looks at his watch. He leans out the window, looking up the street. He returns to typewriter one, types a line or two. He laughs. Then he types on two, then three. He laughs again. He looks at his watch. He goes to the fridge, gets a beer. He opens it. He goes to one of the suitcases, opens it. He rummages through it — women's clothes, and then, what he's looking for — a copy of

9

National Geographic magazine. Mark sits down on the couch, reads. The door lock clicks open. Lee, a woman in her late twenties, enters. Her arms are full of groceries. Mark keeps reading.

LEE. Hello? (*No answer. Lee sets down the bags, starts filling the fridge with the groceries.*) Zucchini. Carrots. Celery. Radishes. Ginger root. Beer. Chocolate eclairs! (*There are no chocolate eclairs.*)

MARK. (*Reading.*) "The main industry of the tribes in the uplands is the cultivation of tea. This work is done only by the women, who laugh and sing as they fill their baskets with the fragrant leaves." I bet the men sit home and write novels. (*Indian accent.*) "Call me Ishmael. Some years ago, having little or no money in my purse. . . ."

LEE. Funny. Mark, make sure you put the magazine back when you're done. It's got those maps in it.

MARK. The maps. Wouldn't want you getting lost out there.

LEE. I got you some food.

MARK. You get a pint of pistachio, maybe? Taco chips?

LEE. Mark, it is so easy. You just slice the vegetables, cover the bottom of the pan with oil . . .

MARK. Little garlic, little ginger, and fry.

LEE. Sauté. It's less trouble than going out, and its cheaper.

MARK. Lee, I am a very big boy. I can find the A & P. Tomorrow morning, I take you to the airport. I come back and first thing, I stock up to ward off the spectre of starvation. A sack of cornmeal, a side of bacon, and a jug of whisky—keep me going for a month.

LEE. Would you please stop teasing me. I'm only trying to . . .

MARK. I am not gonna get fat and cancerous without you. O.K.?

LEE. O.K.

MARK. Everything's pretty expensive there, hah?

LEE. The A & P?

MARK. (*Holding up the National Geographic.*) Ceylon.

LEE. Sri Lanka, my dear, as you know damn well. You're only calling it that to drive me crazy, and I tell you, it won't work! Neo-colonialist pig! I am going to an independent free state, the little island teardrop below the mighty continent of India.

MARK. Where the women wear nose rings, and the men sit around telling dirty stories about visiting anthropologist ladies.

"Crawl in your tent tonight, missy?"

LEE. (*Gestures toward typewriters.*) You've been writing too many of those things.

MARK. Don't I know it. But seriously folks, the man in the magazine says an egg cost him fifty centavos American, and that was in . . . (*Mark checks the date of the Geographic.*) . . . seventy-seven.

LEE. I got my ticket, and I like rice. I told you they advanced me three months salary. I'll manage.

MARK. Good. Cause I doubt there's gonna be any care packages. . . . I called Air India today. Morbid curiosity. Its up over a thousand one way. And then there's living there. How *do* the carefree natives do it?

LEE. Mirrors?

MARK. The correct answer is "They grow their own."

LEE. I know my line. I just don't feel like saying it. Mark — I don't want to go through it all again.

MARK. We've *been* through it, right? *I'm* still going through it, that's all.

LEE. What do you want? One more time, playback the whole routine? I get the call from Professor Buckner, I tell him I won't go without you, he says the university won't pay for lovers of the field workers to tag along. Then I say no to it all, you feel guilty and tell me "It's the opportunity of a lifetime!" I call back and say yes yes I will yes and then we lay the maps out all over the floor, and we dream for me about Dondra Head, and Adam's Peak, and we make love in the maps, and my ass covers Southeast Asia entirely, and then I say I'll still love you when I come back and you believe me. And you tell me the same thing and I even believe you. And then we still have five months of hassle to go. We've been there, Mark. I love you. I'm going.

MARK. O.K.

LEE. O.K.?

MARK. I said, O.K. All you got was vegetables?

LEE. Beer.

MARK. Airfare to Bombay, another plane to Trivandrum, boat to Colombo, plus the bus or jeep or whatever they got to Matara. If I had it, I could pay rent here for twenty years, in advance.

LEE. If *we* had it, we'd be packing your suitcase, and be drink-

11

ing palm wine on the beach tomorrow.

MARK. Here's to us. (*Drinks.*) We don't. (*A silence.*)

LEE. Mark, listen, I quit today. Gave Chuckie-boy no days notice.

MARK. I never liked you working that job.

LEE. It was just waiting tables. (*Lee hands Mark a small stack of bills.*) Tips were good this week. I want to leave something towards next month.

MARK. I told you. I don't want you helping out if you're not here.

LEE. I'm here.

MARK. You got a seven o'clock plane in the morning. I am not gonna spend this tonight. (*Mark puts the money down on the table. Nobody touches it for a moment. Then Lee shrugs, puts it back in her purse. She looks over at the row of typewriters.*)

LEE. How's the junk factory going?

MARK. Slow. Rothman called today.

LEE. What'd he want?

MARK. He wanted to tell me he's got guys off the street waiting to write these things for two hundred bucks apiece. Says I take too long, make them too fancy. Says if he wanted art, he'd buy a Picasso.

LEE. So?

MARK. So I told him I'd get 'em in faster. Then, as soon as I hung up, I couldn't write another goddamn word. I sat around playing "why the hell am I doing this?"

LEE. Food and shelter?

MARK. I was thinking of guys like Ralph. He gets by. Doing some half-ass version of his writing for money never enters his head. Someday the world will grasp the significance of his perceptual alphabet poems, and the giants of literature will crawl to kiss his unwashed feet.

LEE. Ralph's work is stupid.

MARK. Yeah, but Ralph's work is stupid cause its stupid, not because he's getting paid for it to be stupid.

LEE. Mark, lighten up. Think of the cheap thrills you're giving people. (*Lee goes to typewriter one, reads off the roll of paper running through it. Reading:*) "The sheik spread Amanda's legs wide, lashing her ankles to the posts of his tent. The curvaceous blonde whimpered with fear, but, in a moment of odd calm, she no-

12

ticed her pert nipples were standing at attention. Sheik Ahmad tweaked one with a horny fingernail. As he shucked off his burnoose he began to sing, 'Give my regards to Broadway, Remember me to Herald Square . . .'" Hmmm. Tell me again, what do you do if you want art?

MARK. Buy a Picasso.

LEE. Right. Aren't you gonna get in trouble with this?

MARK. I get bored.

LEE. You're hopeless, you know. What's the title of this one?

MARK. Lust in Beirut.

LEE. (*Pointing to typewriters two and three.*) And?

MARK. Lust in London. Lust in Las Vegas.

LEE. Beautiful. How's the novel going?

MARK. Hey, now that you asked, you know that second chapter you didn't like—I reworked the entire thing. (*Mark goes to a drawer, takes out a thick manuscript.*) You wanna hear it?

LEE. Not right now, O.K.? I'd rather just talk to you. (*Mark replaces the manuscript in the drawer.*)

MARK. Great. You'll hear it in a year.

LEE. Will you take it easy?

MARK. I just want you to be sweet to me.

LEE. I'm sorry, babe. I know it makes some money, but when I look at the stuff in those typewriters, everything connected with writing drives me up the wall. She likes it. That's sick.

MARK. Who?

LEE. What's her name. The blonde. Amanda. Maybe it wouldn't bug me so much if it paid more.

MARK. You want me to wait tables? That pays more. Maybe I can get your old job. Its too bad everybody can't go to Sri Lanka, all expenses paid.

LEE. Mark, I told you I'd stay. I'll tear up the ticket. Do you still want that?

MARK. I'd feel guilty forever, and you know it. Besides, what would the neighbors say? "She stayed home to support that asshole." I love you, that's all—and I don't want you to leave. I know you're going.

LEE. Mark, I don't want to leave you either. . . .

MARK. Well, we all agree on that one, sort of. (*Mark goes to the fridge.*) Beer?

LEE. Sure. (*Mark takes out two beers, opens them.*)

13

MARK. I believe I'll have one myself.

LEE. (*Noticing his other beer near the typewriter.*) Hey, you've already got one.

MARK. So I do. So I do. (*Mark hands Lee her beer, picks up his old one. He has one in each hand. The lights fade.*)

> *Lights up in a dingy hallway, bare fluorescents, yellowing linoleum. Herman the messenger approaches two apartment doors at the hallway's end. In another area of the stage, lights are dim on Mark and Lee in their apartment.*
>
> *Herman looks as before, except that the package he was carrying is now hidden under his ragged topcoat. He takes out the package, leans it up carefully against the wall. Herman's door is the furthest from Mark and Lee, as he has the apartment next door to theirs. Herman points to his door.*

HERMAN. Home again, home again, jiggity jog. Early to bed and early to rise. This is good, as I will have a test tomorrow, and must answer. (*Herman holds up two fingers.*) Messenger test number two. (*Herman holds up one finger.*) Test number one was my Pony Express Messenger Service Beginner Messenger Test. Miss Brickell from the home made me wash very hard. Then she drove me in the Director's car to find the office and Mr. Ginetti in a great state of ugliness, as it remains today. It is green inside and many black youths and Mr. Ginetti lounge about smoking drugs and cursing in joking fun. There are, and were, however, photographs of naked women touching themselves with pleasure, and with large breasts, which I am fond to see. So that there was an appealing prospect, as well as freedom, leading me on. Mr. Ginetti gave me the Messenger Test Number One, in which I must find a place to which he sends me, though not to pick up or deliver. He wrote on a piece of paper. I still have this paper, as it is a souvenir of success. (*Herman takes a crumpled piece of paper from his coat pocket, unfolds it, and reads.*) "Baskin-Robbins, 273 West Fourteenth. Ask for Hector." Hector was a Spanish person and rude. He wished to know why I asked for him. I showed him my note. He said "You crazy or something." Then he remembered the test, and called Mr. Ginetti. He said to the telephone, "He's here." I clapped my hands like this. (*Herman*

14

claps his hands, and jumps up and down.) I passed. Which was the first step of the journey that leads me to this violence, which first I do, and then explain. (*Herman takes a rock out of his pocket.*) Rock. (*Herman hits himself sharply on the forehead with the rock. He cries out with the pain. He bleeds. He wipes the blood onto his face and coat, then throws the rock away. He holds up two fingers.*) Tomorrow, Messenger Test Number Two. Mr. Ginetti will question, "Where is the package?" I will say "The delivery was stolen from me by evil gangsters in combat," and I will display my injury. I will be believed and pass the test, as I have never lost a package before, and as I work for very little money and so am a valuable employee, and chiefly as I am an idiot person and not one to deceive normals. By these acts the package will belong to yours truly, and I hope there is inside an object worth perhaps fifty dollars from Mr. Edelstein at Buy and Sell Store to put in my coffee cans, and so to sooner stop messenger work, and instead of moving things to move myself about on earth, which is called going there and not messenger service.

Later I will open and see it. But travel business first. Tonight cancel Hotel Excelsior Madrid. Book Orient Express Vienna-Istanbul. Book Air Nepal New York-Katmandu. Call Hertz.

I have been myself, by my current possible method, to Macao, Belize, Padang, Rangoon, Dakar, Yap, Paramaribo, Dijibouti, Zomba, Ulan Bator, Lhasa, and Gangtok. Why not Paris, Los Angeles, and Albany are you thinking? Too easy to get there. I am handling complex itineraries with my telephone and map.

Let me now let myself in in silence so as not to disturb the neighbors. (*Herman takes out his key, picks up his package, lets himself in to his apartment very quietly. He's gone behind his door. Lights fade.*)

Lights up in Mark and Lee's apartment. Mark and Lee are on the couch, his head in her lap. A few empty beer bottles are on the table in front of them, along with a bottle of Jack Daniels and two half-full glasses. It is night outside the window. Lee leans forward, trying not to disturb Mark, picks up her drink. Mark sits up suddenly, shakes his head to clear it.

MARK. Quiet here tonight, hah. A little too quiet. Probably been a death-ray attack while I was sleeping. Streets littered with corpses. (*Mark goes to the window, looks out.*) Nope. Business as usual. How come the phone isn't ringing with everybody saying goodbye?

LEE. I said goodbye to everybody. (*Dim glow of a neon barsign blinks on outside the window.*)

MARK. Damn Leroy turned his sign on. I told him to keep it dark tonight, in honor of your passing.

LEE. I don't even know him. I've been in that bar once, to use the john. Creepy, to say the least.

MARK. Too true. (*Silence for a long moment. Then Mark's hands go up to his face, his fingers forming the eyepiece of a periscope. His head swivels as he looks through it, inspecting the sea.*) Ah! I knew it. Enemy carrier. That deceptive calm always signals danger. (*Into a beer bottle microphone.*) Forward torpedo room? Ready?

LEE. (*Not yet eager to play.*) Ready.

MARK. (*German accent.*) Gut. Lieutenant, take over the periscope and give me a range on her.

LEE. (*Miming periscope.*) Mein Kapitan! That is a hospital ship. Unmistakeable. The red cross on its side. The Geneva Convention forbids any. . . .

MARK. Don't talk to me about the Geneva Convention! This is war! Give me that scope! (*Mark looks through the scope formed by Lee's hands.*) Enemy carrier. Look again, Lieutenant, if you don't want to find yourself on latrine duty at Dachau. (*Lee looks again through her scope.*)

LEE. Carrier, fifteen hundred yards and closing. . . .

MARK. (*Into beer bottle mike.*) Torpedo room! Load one!

LEE. One thousand yards and closing. . . .

MARK. Flood one!

LEE. Seven hundred fifty yards and closing. . . .

MARK. FIRE EIN! (*They wait tensely, and then they rock as the shock waves of the explosion hit the submarine.*)

LEE. (*Still at scope.*) She's burning. Right on the crosshairs. Like a toy ship . . . burning of a painted ship upon a painted ocean.

MARK. I'm sure the poetry does you credit, Lieutenant, but destroyers will be here any moment. Take her down to fifty fathoms.

LEE. Fifty fathoms!

MARK. You question my orders, lieutenant? We'll soon see

what this bucket of bolts is made of! (*Mark laughs maniacally. The doorbell rings.*) Depth charge signal! Take her down faster!

LEE. We've sprung a leak! (*Lee moves toward the door.*) Bulkheads number seven and eight are giving way! (*The doorbell rings again.*) It must be Crystal. I asked her over. I wanted to see her before I left.

MARK. I thought you said your goodbyes.

LEE. Not this one. (*Lee opens the door and Crystal enters. She is a blonde, in her late twenties, wearing a nurse's uniform under her coat. They embrace.*) You coming from work?

CRYSTAL. Yeah. Just got off.

LEE. Our sub was sinking when you rang. Saved us both.

CRYSTAL. You guys still play those games?

LEE. Only when Mark cons me into it.

CRYSTAL. I could never think that fast.

MARK. You don't think. You let the words fall outta your mouth. My specialty. (*Crystal embraces Mark as well.*)

CRYSTAL. Marko, how you doing?

MARK. O.K. The flag still waves. How're my brothers on Ward Six?

CRYSTAL. O.K. Some of 'em, anyway.

MARK. Any fights today?

LEE. Mark, do you really want the details?

MARK. I asked, didn't I?

LEE. You're just goofing with it.

CRYSTAL. It doesn't bother me. I'm *there*, you know. This is just telling.

LEE. O.K. Give him the gory details.

CRYSTAL. You remember Vincent, the old one? He was playing with himself again. Trying to make everyone stare at him.

MARK. It work?

CRYSTAL. Only on me. The rest of them are way past that sort of thing. They sat around today, mostly. The ones I call the trees did their usual number, swaying back and forth.

MARK. Ah! The vegetable life! I'm looking forward to it. Forty years to go. Lemme show you my future brothers and sisters, keeping cool. (*Mark goes to the fridge, takes out a bunch of celery, waves it at Crystal and Lee. Pointing to each stalk in turn.*) Bruce, Ralph, Nigel, Kitty, Tiffany, Sabrina, and Kelly.

17

LEE. Mark, come down, will you?

MARK. O.K., I'm a little wired by the situation here, the fog's thick, but I believe I can see the runway.

CRYSTAL. (*To Lee.*) All packed, hah?

LEE. Yeah. This morning.

MARK. Lee's ready. Can't wait to spread her wings.

LEE. Mark, please. Can't you just be happy for me?

MARK. I am happy for you. I am also jealous.

LEE. Professor Buckner is sixty-seven years old. He does not want to get into my pants.

MARK. Why not?

LEE. Maybe I've lost the magic. Maybe he's . . . Why am I answering your dumb questions?

MARK. Don't ask me. I'm not jealous of Buckner. I'm jealous of *you*, having your own work set out in front of you on a plate — nothing holding you back. Even if you try to bang your head against it, the wall's gone.

LEE. That's your wall, Mark.

MARK. I didn't build it.

LEE. Who the hell did? The big bad world? Me? Aren't you the man who told me thinking was the only way to travel — that anywhere you go, you drag your ass with you?

MARK. It's heavier at home.

CRYSTAL. Mark?

MARK. Yeah?

CRYSTAL. You're whining.

MARK. Crystal, can't two people bitch at each other decently with you around?

CRYSTAL. Not you two. Christ, I thought you guys had this worked out. You sound like three months ago.

LEE. We have it worked out.

CRYSTAL. Un huh. Tell me another.

LEE. Come on, Crys. Hey, where's Jeff? I thought maybe you'd bring him over.

CRYSTAL. He's staying over a friend's. They're taking him to school in the morning. Mother's night out. Oh yeah, he wants to know what you're gonna bring him.

LEE. From Sri Lanka?

CRYSTAL. Where else you going?

LEE. I don't know if they have anything there a seven year old boy would be interested in . . . but I'll do my best. (*A moment of silence. Crystal starts to cry. She hugs Lee again.*) Crys . . .

CRYSTAL. Silly, hah.

LEE. Yes. I'm not leaving forever. I'll be back in this room in twelve months. Just have some good times, write me some letters, Jeff grows up a little more, and I'm back.

CRYSTAL. Now you're being silly. A year is a long time. You can forget everything in twelve months. I know a nurse did it in six. She was on the ward like me, and then she was *in* it. She was so nuts she thought she was still working. Kept asking for her check.

MARK. Not all that nuts.

CRYSTAL. She didn't get it.

MARK. At least she was asking.

CRYSTAL. Lee, I just keep thinking you're gonna come back different.

LEE. Crystal, you've been my best friend for fifteen years. Do you think I'm not gonna love you anymore because I went somewhere?

CRYSTAL. No—I guess I'm just happy for you and sad for me. I had this dream last night—you were real tan, and didn't recognize me. Mark, you're not gonna grow a beard, are you?

MARK. In mourning, you mean? I wasn't thinking of it.

CRYSTAL. Good. I want us to look exactly the same when she gets off the plane.

MARK. Maybe a small one . . . a Van Gogh. Watch out for them crows over the wheatfield, baby!

LEE. You'd look terrible.

MARK. Could be. Ladies, drink away your troubles. (*Mark raises his drink.*)

CRYSTAL. Yeah. (*All drink. Crystal wanders over to the typewriters.*) This the porno stuff? (*Mark grabs her, leads her away from the typewriters.*)

MARK. You're too young to be exposed to such filth.

CRYSTAL. Hey, let go of me. I'm curious about your work.

MARK. That is not my work. That's how the rent gets paid. Hopefully. (*Crystal shakes free of Mark. She takes a look at one of the sheets of typing, reads. Mark opens the drawer for his novel manuscript.*) Crystal, I'd appreciate your disinterest. You asked about my work? The novel is going fine.

19

CRYSTAL. Kid, listen to your mother. Doing this stuff is no good for your head.

MARK. (*Closing the manuscript drawer.*) Not to worry. Once this novel is out I get into the true art form of the eighties—retailing. Major motion pictures will be offered to me—by telephone. I'll speak at college graduations, tell them about the virtues of hard work. Then—late in life—politics.

CRYSTAL. This novel I been hearing about for so long, Marko—What is it? Romance? Adventure? Mystery?

MARK. Not really.

CRYSTAL. I dig mysteries to read in bed. I bet you got one with some really crazy twist I'll never guess.

MARK. You're out of luck.

CRYSTAL. Come on, Mark. You won't let anyone but Lee read any of it. What's it about?

LEE. Go ahead, Mark. I want to hear this too.

MARK. My book is about a man who's trying to write a book. The book *he's* trying to write is about this man, see, who's trying to write a book. That man's book is about . . .

LEE. Mark, cut the crap, please. Be straight about it for once.

MARK. O.K. The book's just about some people hanging around on the planet, trying to find out how to live and be happy—plus there's major digressions on clocks, dancing, mirrors and death.

CRYSTAL. That's not what I wanted to know. What I want to know is, what happens.

MARK. You can read it when it's done.

CRYSTAL. I been hearing that one for three years.

MARK. I told you what it was about.

CRYSTAL. Yeah. How to live. Does the boy author know the answers to that one?

MARK. I know the questions by heart.

CRYSTAL. Even I know the questions, and I'm not writing a book about it.

MARK. All right. I guess I'm just trying to tell people what I've seen and dreamed—kind of word window in the skull. You know Peter Lorre? Great German actor, came to Hollywood and became a hack with an accent in a bunch of sentimental thrillers. I saw him once on the Ed Sullivan show when I was seven. I remember Ed was introducing him and I knew he didn't sing or dance or tell jokes. I couldn't imagine what he was gonna do. Peter Lorre walked out there, sat on a stool, and did this monologue of a man with a glass head. Anyone can see inside, and his thoughts are there, in pictures, like dreams. Embarrassing. So, he wears a hat. Always. He's an artist — sensitive, unappreciated, broke. He hates the vulgar, pedestrian people around him. One day the wind blows off his hat. It's gone. He's gotta get home. He gets on a bus, and a real prim old lady is looking at him funny. He's thinking how he'd like to bury a hatchet in her face and watch her bloody forehead split in two — and the old lady screams. She can see him, murdering her in his head. She's freaking out, and everyone on the bus rises up, staring into his head, ready to kill the little monster. He's terrified. He runs. He makes it home to his little room. He sits there at the mirror, staring into the red fever swirling in his skull.

Ten years later *I'm* riding a bus and I finally get it. He didn't have a glass head. He believed that other people knew his thoughts, and this forced him to confront his own bloody and useless mind *at every moment*. So, he cracked, or maybe he faced it all and came through. I don't know. I do know he had a head just like yours or mine. Except Peter Lorre's face was on it. . . . Why did I tell that story?

CRYSTAL. I was asking about your book, cause you're so damn shy about it. So I was asking, O.K.?

MARK. O.K. I was answering.

LEE. Is that true, Mark? Peter Lorre on TV and all?

MARK. Yeah. That's true, or how I remember it anyway.

CRYSTAL. Mark, you really plan to pay the rent and food and all with those jerk-off manuals?

MARK. Please. The publishing world is sensitive, especially Leisure Books, and its subsidiaries — Bizarre Books and Playtime Classics.

LEE. I've been telling him, Crys, the market for sex books is going to dry up. Its a new age, you know.

MARK. The purchasers of Leisure books have not yet heard that joyful trumpet. It's hard to figure out fifty-seven varieties with your hand. They still need me. Besides, I've got another chicken in the pot. Lee, I didn't tell you. Once you go, I'm gonna use that space where your desk was to install my recombinant DNA laboratory. Soon as the new life forms are rolling off the production line, me and them will sing all together,

"We're in the money!" Then I plan to buy Sri Lanka and turn it into a Disneyland version of itself; fake cities, fake street peddlers, fake tribal life, and fake anthropologists. You want another drink?

CRYSTAL. Lee, we going out or not?

MARK. Out?

LEE. Mark, I'm touched. You're so possessive, now that I'm leaving. We're just going for an hour or so. Girl talk. You've been obnoxious anyway, so don't make a face. . . . All right. We'll have one more for the road.

MARK. All right! What would you like, my dears? We got beer. Also, half a bottle of Jack, unwatered by the maid.

CRYSTAL. Jack Daniels and water.

LEE. I'll have the same.

MARK. Baby makes three.

CRYSTAL. Mark, you got a cigarette? I'm out.

MARK. It's gonna be a Lucky. Macho's last gasp.

CRYSTAL. I know what it is. Gimme one. (*Mark lights Crystal's cigarette. All three sit, smoke and drink.*)

MARK. So you girls are going out, hah? Where you going?

LEE. We are going to drink kamikazis at the Second Chance.

MARK. Fancy. You sure you're not going out on the stoop to sing and drink beer?

CRYSTAL. We ain't done that since that night two years ago. I was never so drunk in my life. Mark, you were on top of a car, on one knee, singing "Earth Angel." We hadda haul you down.

MARK. Maybe we should give a farewell concert.

LEE. I'm ready.

MARK. You want to do "Stay?"

LEE. That's your number. I don't know it so well.

MARK. You're the back-up. It's just oooooh ooooooh, and then the bridge is that doodoodoodooot, doodoodoodooot, doodoo-doodooooot . . .

LEE. All right. Let's go, on a wing and a prayer. (*Silence. To Mark:*) It's you. Go. (*Lee sings the doo-wop back-up as Mark sings lead.*)

MARK and LEE. (*Sing.*)*

*STAY by Maurice Williams © 1960 CHERIO CORP. International Copyright secured. All rights reserved. Used by permission. (See *MUSIC NOTE.*)

Why don't you stay, just a little bit longer
Please please please please, say that you're going to
Now your mommy won't mind, and your daddy won't mind
If you have another dance, yeah, just one more tiiime . . .
(*Crystal dances a sexy step as the singing continues.*)
CRYSTAL. My sister taught me this one by putting me on top
of her feet. (*Crystal joins in with Lee and Mark. Their singing is fine; strong clean harmony.*)
LEE, CRYSTAL, MARK. (*Sing.*)
Stay! Just a little bit longer
Please please please please, say that you will
Put your sweet lips to mine, say that you'll love me
All of the tiiime. Stay! just a little bit longer
Why don't you stay, just a little bit longer
Why don't you *STAY!*
(*Applause from outside the apartment door. Lee opens the door, and Eddie enters. He wears dark glasses, an old leather jacket, a pair of greasy jeans. He's carrying a shopping bag. He embraces Lee.*)
EDDIE. Not bad.
LEE. The song? Or me?
EDDIE. Both. Hey, Marko! I figured, last night of love, didn't want to come over and interrupt in mid-hump, but I see you got company anyway. I was gonna drop in this afternoon, but this guy José in my building gave me these pills, and as I ain't working tomorrow I took 'em. Then I drank some of that rotten green beer they got down at the Kokomo, till everybody in the place started to look like the face on the Captain Krunchy cereal box. So I'm coming over, and I walked out, got on my bike, and I lunched it in a fucking pothole. When I could stand up, I see the fucking engine is burning. Nice little fire all over it. I was trying to call the pothole commissioner like a good citizen, but my face kept hitting the glass on the phone booth. So, I gave up on that one, got the machine to a garage, and I sold it for parts. I was almost crying. I had that bike for five years. So I got on the BMT and I nodded out, and when I opened one eye the train was going over a fucking bridge. I ended up in fucking Astoria. So, I'm late to say goodbye. (*Eddie eyes Crystal, gestures toward her. To Lee:*) Who?
LEE. My friend Crystal. Crystal, this is Eddie. (*Eddie walks over to Crystal, looks her in the eye.*)

EDDIE. Want to? I hope I'm not outta line here, in a living room and all, but nurses drive me crazy. (*Eddie holds his head in both hands.*) Ooooh. I never shoulda taken those gorilla biscuits. Mind if I sit down? (*Eddie sits next to Crystal. She gets up, moves across the room. Eddie shrugs. Crystal is staring at him, trying to figure out what he is.*)

CRYSTAL. Lee, this joker is a *friend* of yours?

LEE. Yeah. An old friend of Mark's, and mine. You gotta know how to handle him.

CRYSTAL. I got practice with lunatics. Watch me. (*To Eddie.*) Hi. I'm Crystal. We're going to talk normally. How are you?

EDDIE. Feeling strange at the moment, but that's no news.

CRYSTAL. (*To Lee.*) See. Its easy if you talk to them calmly. (*To Eddie.*) Edward, what do you do? I mean, are you working?

EDDIE. I'm driving a van, but I figure to become a soldier of fortune.

CRYSTAL. A what?

EDDIE. A merc. A guy who fights for money. I'm learning it.

CRYSTAL. To fight? Like in the street?

EDDIE. Like with real bullets in foreign countries for whoever pays.

CRYSTAL. You're learning? You go to school?

EDDIE. I'm teaching myself, from books. I'm studying sentry removal now, working at home. I got a dummy.

CRYSTAL. Great. Mark, is this guy for real?

MARK. They don't come any realer.

EDDIE. I'm also doing a correspondence course on fire technology. "Arson: Theory and Technique." I'm gonna learn explosives next. You satisfied?

CRYSTAL. No. Where'd you learn to run your mouth at women like . . .

EDDIE. Hey! Enough quiz from blondie here. Lee, I brought you something. (*Eddie takes a bouquet of flowers out of his shopping bag.*) Bon voyage bouquet.

LEE. Eddie, that's really sweet.

EDDIE. Damn right it is. Listen, tell me something about Sri Lanka. I went to the library around the corner from me to look it up, but they had no books or anything.

LEE. Well, it's hot, with a lot of jungle. The people are Indian, mostly Hindus. And something else. No crime. Anywhere.

24

EDDIE. Nothing? Not even a little . . .

LEE. No. Except by the occasional foreigner, and they don't even have a jail to put him in.

EDDIE. Uh oh. Low crime rate is a sign of bad times. Means there's nothing worth stealing.

LEE. Maybe they think that nothing you can steal is worth anything.

EDDIE. Gimme that again.

MARK. Lee's just getting fancy with you. She means they don't believe in it. They're nice.

EDDIE. Ah hah. That's great. They don't have to worry about losing their TV's out the window.

LEE. They don't have TV.

EDDIE. No kidding.

MARK. What's the big deal? Neither do we.

LEE. Hey, Crys, we better get going if we're going.

EDDIE. Crystal, I gotta tell you before you go. You make me drip just looking at you.

CRYSTAL. Is he serious?

EDDIE. Why do fools fall in love?

CRYSTAL. Lee, let's get out of here. I don't think he's funny. In a moment I'm gonna take a hammer to that bulge in his jeans.

EDDIE. Today I destroyed a tank shift Indian Scout, which is a machine it is impossible to replace for money, and now my heart is broken. Why don't you bitches leave? Mark and me have things to talk over.

LEE. I been wanting to get out of here anyway.

CRYSTAL. Yeah. It's getting scuzzy.

EDDIE. You girls smoke two and eat four for me, hah.

LEE. Be good. (*Lee and Crystal exit.*)

MARK. Drink?

EDDIE. Don't mind if I do. (*Lights fade.*)

Lights up on Herman's apartment. Two doors, one to a bathroom, the other to the building's hallway. Telephone, bed, dresser, table, chair, kitchen sink, some clothes scattered about. Very simple, very sloppy. A rear window, as in Mark and Lee's apartment. Outside that window, night. Dim pink light of the same neon bar sign. There is a Playboy playmate on the wall. There is a picture of Jesus on the wall. There is also a grade-

school window shade type map, with a pull-down roll for each continent. South America is showing. There is also a bookshelf, filled with National Geographics and cheap pornographic novels. The package is on a table. Herman is on the phone.

HERMAN. (*On the telephone.*) A continental. . . . Yes. *Lincoln* continental. . . . Oh, no. I am not allowed to drive a moving car. . . . Yes. Someone very nice please. . . . Right. Montevideo airport on the twenty-fourth. . . . Thank *you*, Kathy. (*Herman hangs up, goes to map, rolls up South America, pulls down Africa. The maps are inked with route lines in different colors. Herman traces one with his finger. He heads for the phone, stops, looks at his watch.*) Pill time. (*He takes his pill bottle from a drawer, takes a pill, puts the pills back in a drawer. He goes to the phone, dials eleven numbers.*) Nairobi Hilton? . . . I can hear you very nicely. Yes. I would like to make a reservation. For two weeks, starting on the twenty-eighth. . . . Do you have an extra big room? . . . That's for Herman, H,E,R,M,A,N. . . . Thank you very much, sir. (*Herman hangs up the phone, looks out at the audience. He goes to the sink, begins to take wet socks out of it, and hang them on a stand-up drying rack.*) Eight hundred numbers. No charge to calling party. That's me. I travel always by this method. If I think it, I am sad that I do not coincide in the body with my reservations. Making them, however, satisfies for now. I have yet to cancel. (*Herman gestures toward the package.*) You see the package? Still unopened. My idea is the same as vegetables. Eat your string beans first, and then funny meatloaf, and *then* you get to eat potatoes with gravy, and the last is first. But you have to be quick, or its cold, because many times the mashed is not as hot as they should be. So, *best* for *last*, and hope you get to it in time. Best to begin is weakness, and for babies, which we are not or we would be in our cribs and praying inside our tiny brains that mother is there in the dark, and to stay dry. So. Not until morning. First, sun up. Then, open. (*Herman hangs up the last sock. Lights on him fade.*)

Lights up on Lee and Crystal at a table in the "Second Chance." Bar noise, music. They have empty glasses, and two fresh kamikazis in front of them.

CRYSTAL. Hey—Lee. I get a little nervous in these places. I told you about it.

LEE. I don't remember. I must have been drunk.

CRYSTAL. We both were drunk, or I wouldn't have told you. You know the people who work in these joints, how they all wear those same T-shirts, and whisper to each other about the customers . . .

LEE. Wait a minute. I worked in one of these places for five years. It is not like that.

CRYSTAL. Lee, I'm not telling you how it is. I'm telling you how I think it is. I know they're people, like me, but they *feel* different. It's like they'd still be dressed up with their clothes off. Like they're enough for themselves, so they don't need anything, so they can never be disappointed.

LEE. Very clear. You sound like Mark. Every time the lights dim when I plug in the iron he says, (*Newscaster voice.*) "Flying saucers, hovering over the power lines in upstate New York, are draining our vital juices . . ."

CRYSTAL. Only I'm not kidding. It's a feeling that nobody's really human but you and the people real close to you.

LEE. Like "everybody's crazy but you and me . . ."

CRYSTAL. You're making fun of me.

LEE. I didn't mean it that way. I'm a little drunk is all.

CRYSTAL. Good. Then I'll tell you that I went to one of those computer dating places once—but I quit.

LEE. You what?

CRYSTAL. You heard me. But I quit before they matched me. I got paranoid. I thought they were all from somewhere else, and they were gonna fix me up with one of *them*. Earth meat. You know those rooftop tennis court bubbles? I read where they found parts of a UFO in one of them. Hey, I saw the photograph, Lee.

LEE. Crystal, I'm gonna miss you. You're nuts.

CRYSTAL. It's one of my best characteristics, along with the good body . . . You're going to the country, right?

LEE. What?

CRYSTAL. Sri Lanka is in the country, isn't it?

LEE. It's all country. There's one city, about like Albany, and a few little towns.

CRYSTAL. Don't get snotty with me. This is Crystal, remember. I knew you when.

LEE. O.K., O.K. I've just described it so many times . . .

CRYSTAL. No excuse. You have never described it to me. So, where was I?

LEE. The country?

CRYSTAL. Right. I looked it up in the encyclopedia. You gotta bring bugspray. They got some big bugs.

LEE. Crys, I am not worrying about bugs. I'm worrying about Mark and me.

CRYSTAL. He loves you, right?

LEE. Right.

CRYSTAL. You love him, right?

LEE. Right.

CRYSTAL. You two are so far ahead of the game, you think you can win, and you worry you won't. Be glad you're doing so good. Write long mushy letters, and stop trying to order something that isn't on the menu right now. You'll go hungry that way, believe me. Live with what you got, and see what happens.

LEE. I know what happens. You know Sheila and David?

CRYSTAL. Assholes. Now they're divorced assholes.

LEE. That is not the point. The point is that they really had something good going with each other, and then he got that job setting up computer systems in Iowa City for four months, and she was in grad school and couldn't go . . .

CRYSTAL. And there was this real cute guy handing out the towels at the health club . . .

LEE. No guy. They came back together, and everything was supposed to be like it was before. But it wasn't. And there wasn't any other guy, or girl, or anything. Just different.

CRYSTAL. So. Things change. People change. You wanna stop that?

LEE. No. I just want them to change my way. Dammit, Crystal, he's such a baby.

CRYSTAL. That's his act. Only fools you . . . Drink up. (*They both drink, as lights dim on them, though they stay visible.*)

> *Lights up on Mark and Eddie, in Mark's apartment. They are also drinking. Both take a drink.*
> *Eddie is at the typewriters, reading, and has gotten about four*

28

feet of paper into "Lust in Beirut," on typewriter one. He's singing "Earth Angel" to himself as he reads.

EDDIE. (*Sings softly.*)
Earth angel, earth angel, will you be mine
My darling dear, love you all the time
I'm just a fool, a fool in love . . .*
MARK. You never learn how that goes. Will you listen for once?
EDDIE. I'm reading.
MARK. Listen anyway. (*Sings.*) "I'm just a fool, a fool in love, with youuuuu ooooh, ahhhhhaaaoooooo." And then back. "Earth Angel, earth angel . . ."
EDDIE. I got it.
MARK. Let's hear it.
EDDIE. I'm reading. (*Eddie reads. Silence for a moment.*) Marko, you are a fucking genius. This stuff is hilarious, and it's giving me a hardon in the bargain.
MARK. Keep quite about "hilarious." Those are not supposed to be satires of porno novels. They are supposed to *be* porno novels.
EDDIE. Yeah, especially this business with the minaret and the monkeys, when she gets her . . .
MARK. I wrote it, remember.
EDDIE. Still writing the novel too, hah?
MARK. Yeah, but it's going around in circles lately. I'm not even sure I understand it anymore.
EDDIE. That's too bad.
MARK. Yeah, isn't it. Try Earth Angel. (*Eddie and Mark sing. Eddie is unsure of the vocal embellishments, and Mark helps him through. Some good harmony, some lousy.*)
EDDIE and MARK. (*Singing.*)
Earth angel, earth angel, will you be mine
My darling dear, love you all the time
I'm just a fool, a fool in love with youuuuu, uh uh ooh
Earth angel, earth angel . . .
MARK. All right!
EDDIE. You know—I like that friend of yours. Crystal.

*Used by permission of Dootsie Williams Publications.

29

MARK. Oh? Then how come you came on to her like you were gonna rape her on the floor?

EDDIE. I figured I'd make an impression. Marko, whatever's got tail at one end . . .

MARK. Got teeth at the other.

EDDIE. Right. You gotta be strong from the beginning.

MARK. Bullshit. The beginning was the end.

EDDIE. You think so? The bigger the iceberg . . .

MARK. The more water when she melts. Look, I know Crystal a long time. She kicked her husband out three years ago. Now maybe she goes out once a month with some doctor from the hospital. She's got a kid too — great kid, Jeffrey, but she's had some rough times with him. Now she's got him in a special program at school, and . . .

EDDIE. Hey. What are you telling me? I'm not good enough for her? I don't work for a fucking living?

MARK. Eddie, take it easy. The two of you should get married, all right. Get a farm in Vermont. I'm just a little crazy tonight is all. . . . Eddie, you got any money?

EDDIE. Sure. Whatever you need. (*Eddie reaches for his wallet.*) I know where to find you. How much?

MARK. You got a few hundred dollars?

EDDIE. Are you kidding? If I had a few hundred dollars I'd be at Cycle World, talking to a man about a machine.

MARK. I'm serious.

EDDIE. So am I. If you needed ten . . . (*Mark looks over at the typewriters.*)

MARK. Three poor little unborn pornographs, gonna have an abortion. I am gonna trash the ugly little fuckers.

EDDIE. What for? You want to borrow money while you chuck the only way you got of making any.

MARK. I got fired this morning. Rothman called me, said he didn't want these anymore. You know what I said? I was that stupid. I said, "What do you expect me to do with them?" He told me to keep jerking off with them. Then he hung up.

EDDIE. So, either you go down there and hit him, or you forget it.

MARK. Uh uh. Rothman was right. I am jerking off with this crap, and a lot of other things besides. I been living off Lee while I been farting around trying to write a novel and she's going to school days and waiting tables at night, and not only do I make her feel guilty about getting a fucking break, but I also have the goddamn nerve to be jealous of her . . .

EDDIE. Hey, listen . . .

MARK. I don't have enough money to make the rent next week. You know what happens when I land a straight job? I go down there with hate rays coming out of my eyes at the boss for interrupting my writing career which is non-existent anyway, and the poor bastard sees I hate him, has no idea why, and I'm fired in three days.

EDDIE. Look, you're broke. O.K. That's no news, and no crime. Do something about it. What's got you is not all that shit you're saying. It's that Lee ain't gonna be here. If she was leaving me, I'd be crying too, believe me.

MARK. Eddie, have a drink and listen.

EDDIE. Did you hear me?

MARK. I heard you. (*Mark pours himself and Eddie a drink.*) When Lee gets back she is gonna have written a brilliant article called, uh, Tribal Dissociation, or Monkeying Around with the Monkey-God, and she's gonna get a fancy teaching job somewhere, and if she still wants me I'm gonna tail after her to some university where . . .

EDDIE. So you got the whole bad trip in your head. Congratulations. Meanwhile, what are you gonna *do*?

MARK. Do?

EDDIE. Yeah, *do*. Get some money, write your fucking novel, and stop whining.

MARK. How, Mr. Wizard? You know how many fucking years I listen to you talk about all the shit you're going to do? How you're gonna become a merc and go get your ass blown off in Swazululand? Did you *do* that?

EDDIE. I was recruited. I was gonna fly over in a week. They closed the war before I got there. My fault they stopped the war?

MARK. Maybe.

EDDIE. Bullshit.

MARK. My fault I don't have any money?

EDDIE. Yeah.

MARK. Man, all you do when you're not working is drink, take your percodans, and watch TV, and you're giving me a lecture. You're like me, brother — just another asshole. Shake. (*Mark*

31

walks toward Eddie, holding out his hand. Eddie doesn't take it. Mark sits down on the couch. He's close to tears.)

EDDIE. Marko, you're just scared. Your feelings are all mixed up and they're making you crazy.

MARK. I need you to tell me that?

EDDIE. You need someone to tell you something. You don't seem able to tell shit from Shinola anymore. Stand up, hah. (*Mark does not move.*) Stand up!

MARK. All right. (*Mark stands, slightly slumped.*)

EDDIE. That is not standing. Stand *up.* (*Mark stands at attention.*)

MARK. What is this? Officer's candidate school?

EDDIE. Fucking A. We're gonna study not letting your feelings jerk you around. You shoulda started working on it when your dog died. When your Momma looks at you funny cause you ain't crying, then you know its moving along. Then when your Momma dies, and you get her in the ground, and pay the bills, and do your crying where and when you need it — then they can do fucking anything to you, and you ain't there.

MARK. That is not much of a life, sir. (*Eddie smacks Mark across the face.*)

EDDIE. Don't talk back to me, you little shit. (*Eddie raises his hand to hit Mark again. Mark runs away, Eddie running after him. Then, Mark's cornered. He turns, ready to fight. Eddie suddenly cowers in fear, weeping and whimpering.*)

MARK. What the hell are you doing? (*Eddie stands.*)

EDDIE. Watching you wallow in it. You wanna hit me?

MARK. Yeah.

EDDIE. Go ahead.

MARK. No.

EDDIE. Go ahead.

MARK. No.

EDDIE. *Go ahead.*

MARK. *No.*

EDDIE. O.K. (*Mark suddenly slaps Eddie hard across the face. Eddie laughs.*) Getting better. Lee'll come back, and maybe she'll love you. Maybe not. But you got to get along without her *now.* Fact. If you keep crawling around with your mouth open, it should be no surprise to a boy with a college degree if someone kicks a turd in. Do something, man. If you don't they're gonna boot you outta here, and repossess your typewriters, and you're gonna be knocking on my lonely door.

MARK. Lonely door?

EDDIE. I'm entitled. You think I'm sitting there in fucking heaven watching the Gong Show. Asshole. Do something.

MARK. What?

EDDIE. How do I know what? If you can't hold a straight job, learn. Go on welfare.

MARK. Sure. Stand in line and prove to the nice lady I can't work cause I'm psychologically disabled.

EDDIE. Then rob a liquor store. They usually got about five hundred in, if you hit 'em right before they close.

MARK. Funny.

EDDIE. You know, you think you're a hard man to satisfy. You're easy. You are satisfied by what's inside your head, even if it never gets out to anyone else. It's like me and Tuesday Weld. I love her, but that's just something I got. She don't got it.

MARK. You ever think she don't want it?

EDDIE. Whatta you know? She ain't so young anymore.

MARK. She's married.

EDDIE. Lies. You probably read that in the Enquirer.

MARK. People Magazine.

EDDIE. You see. Unreliable source. If that was in the Enquirer —heartbreak. (*Mark begins to pace the room rapidly, pacing and talking.*)

MARK. You know these fantasies you get about robbing some-one—but you're scared to do it cause you'll get caught, and then you think of one where you're really unlikely to get caught, and that makes it actually tempting and you think about it?

EDDIE. Yeah.

MARK. I got one. (*Lights down on Eddie and Mark. Lights up on Herman in his apartment next door. He speaks to the audience.*)

HERMAN. Doing both hearing study and sex reading makes a person who can think different things while making deliveries, such as if a girl with large breasts passes a messenger in his working streets, then I am able to think sexual thoughts that I have learned and do not disturb her walking with my personal attentions such as speaking, as I know through bitter trial and approach to this sticking place that the eyes of women can teach

33

me disgust and hatred of my own shape and being. So I no longer speak to ladies but feed this part of me with reading. Thus my library, all favorites of Mary Fivefingers and her sister Jane, purchased at Black Jack's Peeporama, where I am known as someone who not only looks, but buys as well.

But hearing study also is needed, and those who do not improve mind do so at their peril of having no new tracks to follow and thus wearing the old till they are ruts and you are stuck. (*Herman holds up a tape cassette and points to it.*) So I prepare for my future plans, and what may come if a truck does not hit me, and I do not die in some other manner, which I have hope I will not, as I see by my eyes everyday that surprising death comes, but just to few. (*Herman inserts the cassette into his portable tape recorder. He straightens his tie. He stands, picks up a battered suitcase. He presses the play button on the recorder.*)

TAPE. (*A sexy oriental woman's voice.*) Third lesson. At the Hotel. Repeat after me. (*Herman stands up straight, holding the suitcase. He takes a step forward.*) Please take my baggage in for me. Ching nin ba wo-mun shing.

HERMAN. (*Dropping suitcase to the floor.*) Ching nin ba wo-mun shing.

TAPE. Where is the desk clerk? Jing lee zai nar?

HERMAN. Jing lee zai nar? (*Herman claps his hands, applauding his own success. He listens intently.*)

TAPE. Have you a double room? Shi zao fong duh shwong?

HERMAN. Shizu . . . fong . . . duh . . . duh . . . Shit!

TAPE. Very good. Fourth lesson. At the Restaurant. Repeat after me. (*Herman rushes to sit down in a chair at the table. He sits, waits nervously. Lights down on Herman, and up on Crystal and Lee at their table in the bar.*)

LEE. Crys, I had a dream the other night where I came back, and the apartment was empty. Mark was just gone, and I went walking down the street, crying. People were staring, and I couldn't stop.

CRYSTAL. Look. What happens happens, and you try to help something along if you like it . . . And then there's always the wisdom of the Marvellettes. "There's a whole lotta fish in the sea, yeah, whole lotta fish in the sea."

LEE. The Marvellettes lied. Then they all committed suicide in a hotel in Philly when the first Beatles record hit number one.

Times had changed and the Marvellettes couldn't face tomorrow.

CRYSTAL. Cowards. But the song's reassuring in a stupid way.

LEE. No. The number of quality fish is *very* small. Most of them are with some babyface thing with legs about thirty feet long, because quality fish are as stupid as the rest of them. And the proof of all that is—I don't see you out dating up a storm.

CRYSTAL. Lee, I've been alone for a long time, and it doesn't hurt much anymore—so I get to be choosy. And now I kiss with my eyes open, so I'm *real* choosy. So, I sit home. Its not bad. Anyway, usually the fucking you get ain't worth the fucking you get.

LEE. Crystal, please. You're dealing with the last romantic here.

CRYSTAL. There's two of us left. If you were a man we could reproduce. (*A moment of silence.*)

LEE. I guess I'm lucky.

CRYSTAL. Even if this trip of yours turns you and Mark into monkeys, you're lucky. You know, I think I still love my ex-husband, the crud. I hope he falls off one of those telephone poles in Arizona and lands on his weak mind. Which reminds me. Who's Eddie?

LEE. You're kidding.

CRYSTAL. Just curious. Perverse taste. You known him long?

LEE. Ever since Mark and I began seeing each other. Eight years.

CRYSTAL. So what's he like, really?

LEE. So what's it to ya, hah?

CRYSTAL. I don't know. Nothing. (*Crystal takes her glass, tosses back her head, and drinks it down. She throws the glass against the wall. She starts to cry.*)

LEE. Whatcha do that for? We're gonna get kicked out of here.

CRYSTAL. So what. You're leaving anyway.

LEE. Crystal, stop crying again, will you. If you cry, I'm gonna cry, and I've run through so many feelings about this already that the words Sri Lanka give me a headache. I don't want to turn around at forty and say "what the hell have I done?" I'm going. (*Crystal stops her crying, wipes her eyes with a napkin.*)

CRYSTAL. Crystal lets it all slop over again. Hey, you gonna get a nose ring like those Sri Lanka women?

LEE. Certainly. I'm getting two. (*Lee looks at her watch.*) We gotta get back.

CRYSTAL. (*Yelling.*) Gar-son!

LEE. Crystal! Shh! Besides, there's no garcon. We have a wait-ress.

CRYSTAL. You know, you're right.

LEE. I'll handle it. (*Yelling.*) Check, bitch!

CRYSTAL. Hey, she coulda heard you . . . (*Lee and Crystal laugh as lights fade in the bar. Lights up on Eddie and Mark in the apartment.*)

MARK. You know these fantasies you get about robbing some-one — but you're scared to do it cause you'll get caught, and then you think of one where you're really unlikely to get caught and that makes it actually tempting, and you think about it?

EDDIE. Yeah.

MARK. I got one.

EDDIE. You're gonna snatch the Hope Diamond and escape on the Goodyear Blimp.

MARK. This is a bit more realistic.

EDDIE. O.K. I'll play. Who?

MARK. My next door neighbor. I don't know his name.

EDDIE. How do you know Mr. X has money?

MARK. He's the kind of guy who wouldn't trust banks. He'd sit on it like a toad. He's a messenger. You've seen guys like him on the street, with a package under one arm — a guy who'd sit in there, eat catfood, and talk to the walls, with all the wrong but-tons buttoned, and his fly open. You read in the papers about how guys like that die in their apartments, and the cops find ten thousand dollars stuffed up in back of the refrigerator.

EDDIE. Crazy people usually got nothing, cause if they got something, somebody just takes it away from them.

MARK. This guy has money in there. I know it. And I know he's not home.

EDDIE. You been timing him with a stopwatch?

MARK. Those walls are not thick, to say the least. I hear his shoes hit the floor when he takes them off. I hear it every time he flushes the toilet. I've heard him go out and come in for eight years. He never comes in before midnight on a weekday.

EDDIE. You gonna rob him?

MARK. I'm talking, that's all.

EDDIE. You say there's money. You say he ain't there. Do it.

36

From the looks of your doorlock, if his is like it, you can be inside in fifteen seconds.

MARK. You're nuts.

EDDIE. Your idea, remember. What are you gonna do? You're gonna have a City Marshal in here, and all your pencils are gonna be out on the street.

MARK. All right. You ready?

EDDIE. Me? Are you crazy?

MARK. You son of a bitch. You're chicken. (*Eddie picks up the National Geographic magazine, reads.*) Eddie, I'm going.

EDDIE. You'll fuck up. (*Mark heads for the door.*) Where you going?

MARK. I told you.

EDDIE. Hey, you sure he's not there?

MARK. I'm sure. (*Eddie stands up.*)

EDDIE. I'd only be this stupid for you.

MARK. What if it's the guy's life savings?

EDDIE. He's working, right? So he ain't gonna starve.

MARK. Good. I don't want anyone starving.

EDDIE. Get a flashlight. And a screwdriver.

MARK. Yeah. Right. (*Mark finds a flashlight in a drawer, then the screwdriver.*) Got it.

EDDIE. O.K. Be a man. Lead the way.

MARK. Me?

EDDIE. Marko, this is your party.

MARK. I'm scared.

EDDIE. You're scared? I haven't done anything like this since I was nineteen. (*Pause.*) Marko, let's sit down. (*They both sit.*) We are acting nuts.

MARK. Are we? (*Blackout.*)

Lights up in Herman's apartment, next door. He is still seated, waiting for his "restaurant" lesson in Chinese.

CASSETTE TAPE. Fourth lesson. At the restaurant. Repeat after me. Waiter! Hwo-jee!

HERMAN. Hwo-jee!

TAPE. Dinner for two, please. Wo-mun yee goong, see-way.

HERMAN. (*Attempting to be suave.*) Wo-mun yee . . . way. Uh oh.

TAPE. Some more wine! Zei li yee dier kai jiou!

HERMAN. Zei kai . . . mai . . . I am not supposed to drink wine, as the stimulators in its chemicals . . .

TAPE. Would you give me the check, please. Rwong yee kan . . . (*Herman clicks off the tape. He takes out another cassette tape, points to it.*)

HERMAN. Tomorrow's walking tape. Songs I admire. (*He changes tapes.*) I am unable to learn more learning this evening, so now to bed, and my newest purchase. (*Herman takes a paperback from the shelf.*) "Lust in Bangkok" by my favorite, Abner Dewitt. (*Herman places the book on his pillow. He takes off his shirt, tie, pants, shoes. He is in his underwear and socks.*) Before bed, I move my muscles about for exercise and pleasantness. (*He does so.*) Then I think about God and Jesus that I love and loves me. (*Herman prays in silence, hands together, looking upward.*) Do you know why Jesus is the best? I have talked with believers and not, and with Islamites and Hindus, and Buddha lovers, who is fat. Only Jesus gives us one death, and then mercy. He will forgive you, which if you are a poor man and the sweat of your brow blinds you with tears as you earn your daily bread, and have evil thinking besides, you appreciate this very much. Forgiveness, and one death. (*Herman gets into bed, props himself up, opens his book. He reads. He yawns. Quiet. Lights fade. The stage is dark. A dim "hallway" light comes up and Eddie and Mark appear under it, stepping out of Mark's apartment. Eddie holds a screwdriver, Mark a flashlight. They step silently, cautiously, toward Herman's door. Blackout.*)

END OF ACT I

*Herman's apartment. Lights very dim on Herman sleeping.
Click of the lock snapping back. A stream of light from the hallway splashes in across the bed from the slowly opening door, and
widens. Shadows of Mark and Eddie fall across the bed. Mark
and Eddie step inside, shut the door behind them. Blackness.*

MARK. You did it!

EDDIE. Shhhh.

MARK. Why are you shusshing me? There's nobody here.
(*Mark and Eddie grope their way forward in the darkness.*)

EDDIE. Shhhh. This is a burglary. We're the burglars. We are
supposed to be quiet. It's expected.

MARK. By who?

EDDIE. Shut up.

MARK. Lemme find the light.

EDDIE. No! He comes back, sees the light, calls the cops from
outside. If he comes in, at least we're running before he's calling.

MARK. Running where?

EDDIE. Just start looking, and don't get fancy. Not where
you'd hide it. Where he'd hide it.

MARK. O.K. (*They begin to search clumsily in the dark.*)

EDDIE. Mark!

MARK. You find it?

EDDIE. Listen.

MARK. I'm listening.

EDDIE. Shhhh. (*Sound of Herman's breathing in the dark. He coughs
in his sleep. Eddie moves cautiously closer to Herman's bed. He reaches
out, touches him. Herman grunts, rolls over.*)

MARK. What?

EDDIE. He's here. Sleeping. We're getting out.

MARK. NO! We won't wake him.

EDDIE. We're getting out, now. (*They begin to back out carefully
in the dark. Mark crashes into a lamp. It bangs onto the floor, glass
breaking. Eddie jumps to avoid it, falls into the drying rack full of wet
socks. Herman wakes. He runs to the light switch, throws it on. Eddie
and Mark are tangled on the floor. Herman is half-awake, confused.*)

HERMAN. Shhh. Not safe here. Port Authority Bus Terminal.
That's the only place you can sleep—till they check your papers.

MARK. What's he saying?

EDDIE. I don't know.

HERMAN. Ching lee zai nar bow. They'll take you to the doctors.

EDDIE. He needs a few shock treatments.

HERMAN. Shhh. (*Eddie and Mark stand up slowly, watching Herman.*)

EDDIE. Let's run for it.

HERMAN. Your name is Mark. You're my neighbor. You live next door. In fourteen.

MARK. I got lost.

HERMAN. Can you read numbers? My door says numbers one and three, for thirteen in numbers.

MARK. I made a mistake.

HERMAN. That is lying. I'm scared of you now, as night is outside, and I know you are robbers. Are you going to kill me?

MARK. That's ridiculous.

HERMAN. Good. (*Herman rushes toward the phone, and starts to speak before and as he picks it up and dials.*) Hello, policemen nine one one is lifesaving and discomforts of robbers in this home who murder me with bombs and poisons! Police! (*Herman finishes dialing and talking. He waits for someone to pick up. He taps his foot as it rings. Mark and Eddie stare at him in amazement.*)

MARK. Eddie, we gotta get out of here.

EDDIE. He knows you. You'd be in the back of a squad car in ten minutes.

HERMAN. (*On phone.*) Police? (*Mark leaps suddenly and grabs Herman, yanks him away from the phone. He holds him tight. Herman is kicking and screaming.*) Monsters! Constables!

EDDIE. Easy with him. I told you to be *a* man, not *the* man.

HERMAN. I am a bonded messenger. I have my papers!

EDDIE. Would you shut up. I'm trying to think.

MARK. (*Holding Herman, who is still struggling toward the phone.*) I'm hanging on while you're thinking!

HERMAN. I am going to tell policemen that you killed me. I am dead and you killed me.

EDDIE. Will you stop putting ideas into my head.

HERMAN. Justice! I will point to you from my grave!

EDDIE. Mark, can you shut him up?

HERMAN. Justice! Murderers! (*Mark tries to clamp a hand over Herman's mouth. Herman bites him, and Mark yells in pain.*)

MARK. You bit me.

HERMAN. You are robbing my house.

MARK. Yeah, I understand that, but it's not like it seems.

HERMAN. What is it like? Beasts of the field! Will you hurt me?

MARK. No. (*Looking at his finger.*) Damn. It's bleeding.

EDDIE. Tie him up. That's a start. I'll find some cord or something. (*Eddie searches for cord.*)

HERMAN. Dental floss. It says on the box three hundred yards. I am not as long as three football fields.

EDDIE. You'd break it. Thanks anyway. (*Finds cord.*) I got it. (*Herman struggles in Mark's grip.*) Hold onto him, dammit. You know, we got a real problem here. We let him go, he calls the cops.

MARK. Whadda we do? Adopt him?

HERMAN. Kill me! That's what you'll do! (*Herman struggles frantically in Mark's grip, as Eddie approaches with the rope, extending his mouth toward the distant telephone.*) Hello, officers and gentlemen! Wo-mun tee yee goong! I am the victim of human monsters!

EDDIE. (*Coming at Herman with rope.*) Here we go! (*Eddie and Mark wrestle Herman down onto the floor, where Mark sits on him as Eddie ties his hands behind his back. Herman squeals and grimaces.*)

HERMAN. Torturers! Bondage lust! Inquisitors! (*They stand Herman up, and tie him to a post of his bed.*)

EDDIE. He's gonna get out of that sooner or later, but at least we can take a breath. Number one—we look for what we came for. (*Eddie and Mark search again for Herman's money. Herman watches them. Mark picks up the book on Herman's bed.*)

MARK. Jesus. This is one of mine.

EDDIE. Money, remember.

MARK. (*Finding bookcase.*) They're all mine. If I got royalties on the damn things this guy could keep me going. My biggest fan.

HERMAN. What are you saying to yourself? Talk to others, and it will not be sickness.

MARK. (*Holding up "Lust in Bangkok."*) Me. I wrote this. I'm Abner Dewitt.

41

HERMAN. You are Mark.

MARK. Abner, too.

HERMAN. You lie to make me love you.

MARK. My fan, I could kiss you, if I didn't have to get busy robbing you.

HERMAN. Abner Dewitt does not write robbings, and only violence of sex, which is loved by the body though mind is often disliking it at once.

MARK. Right, my fan. So I do. You should read my novel sometime.

HERMAN. Is it of sex and distant places?

MARK. Not exactly.

EDDIE. Marko, I hate to interrupt, but we are trying to do something really quite simple here. Look, and find.

MARK. Right. (*Eddie and Mark search. As they do so, Herman calls out to them, attempting to misdirect. He is in earnest.*)

HERMAN. (*As Eddie nears his cache.*) Colder! Colder! Even colder! No! You're like ice!

EDDIE. Aha! (*He's found a stack of coffee cans. He shakes each one. One of them tinkles. Eddie opens it, as Herman and Mark watch in silence. Eddie counts money.*) Thirty bucks, and change. (*Eddie tosses the money to Mark.*) Here.

MARK. That's it?

EDDIE. I'm afraid we've already hit the mother lode.

HERMAN. That is my life savings and the help to my future travels so do not insult it. You and your gang will be shut in Sing Sing with violence in your teeth. Black people with muscles will lift weights about you, and white people with broken teeth will snarl. You will rattle your little tin cup along the bars, and it will be in vain, for your mommy will not hear you, and neither will I. They will put you in the Bus Terminal, with no tips, and not let you sing through the wall. (*Herman sings a doo-wop back-up in a slow repetitive monotone, the singing growing softer till it is a low humming.*) Doo-wop do doo-wop, do doo-wop do do do do do do do, doo-wop do doo-wop do do do do . . .

EDDIE. (*Aside to Mark.*) We leave him here, he wiggles out, calls the cops, we both get busted. You get a suspended sentence as a good citizen first timer, and you miss saying goodbye to

Lee. No tragedy. Not so good for me, though. I have taken two falls before, and this could mean five to ten. A serious portion of my life, which I will not part with.

MARK. All right. So I got us in trouble. Do we throw him out the window or what?

EDDIE. Hey man, we are not even *thieves*. For a start, let's get out of his place.

MARK. What about him?

EDDIE. He's gotta come along. (*Mark goes over to Herman.*)

MARK. What's your name?

HERMAN. Herman.

MARK. O.K., Herman. You think you can be quiet now? We're gonna take you next door.

HERMAN. Goody. Visiting. (*Herman springs suddenly, having wriggled his ropes off the bedpost, though his hands are still tied behind his back. He rushes for the door. Mark tackles him.*) You'll fry for this!

EDDIE. Herman, quiet down, and get dressed.

HERMAN. Look ma, no hands.

MARK. Sit down. (*Mark gets Herman to the bed with Eddie's help. Mark finds his pants, struggles to get them on him. It's like trying to dress a recalcitrant baby. No luck. Herman is still in his underwear.*)

HERMAN. My pills! Doctor says, go nowhere without pills. (*To Mark.*) In the drawer. They're green. (*Eddie opens the drawer, takes out the pills, puts them in his pocket.*)

EDDIE. I got 'em. (*Eddie notices the package on the table.*) What's this?

HERMAN. Morning delivery. Don't touch. Pony Express will . . .

EDDIE. Let's take it along.

HERMAN. I'll see you burn in hell for robbing me. (*Eddie picks up the package. Mark begins again to try to get Herman's pants on. While he does so, Eddie, out of idle curiosity pushes the "on" button on Herman's cassette player. Fifties doo-wop rock and roll. Eddie does a little dance, grins.*)

MARK. Jesus. (*Eddie clicks it off.*)

EDDIE. Get his pants on him and let's get out of here.

MARK. Give me a hand, dammit. (*Eddie and Mark together begin to get Herman's pants on him. Lights fade to black.*)

Lights rise on Lee and Mark's apartment. Crystal and Lee have returned. They're drinking bourbon. Lee pours, takes out the ice tray.

LEE. One lump or two?
CRYSTAL. I want all I can get, if you don't mind.
LEE. Let's do another number.
CRYSTAL. Another number. You know "Blanche?"*
LEE. Let's hear it.
CRYSTAL. (*Sings.*) This is the story, of a boy and a girl. . . .
LEE. (*Interrupting.*) Don't care for it. Too philosophical. Let's render that Don Julian and the Meadowlarks classic, "Heaven and Paradise."*
CRYSTAL. I'll take the ba-ba-ba-booms. Where's your lover and his boyfriend?
LEE. Took a walk, maybe?
CRYSTAL. Your last night, and they go out and get pissed in some bar.
LEE. Disgusting.
CRYSTAL. Typical.
LEE. Ready?
CRYSTAL. I am beyond ready.
LEE. All right! One, two, three and a . . .
CRYSTAL. Ba, ba, ba boom . . .
LEE and CRYSTAL. (*Sing.*)
Ba doom, ba ba, ba ba, ba boom
Heaven and Paradise, uh oh oh
Ahh, oh—
(*Scuffling and bumping from outside the door to the hallway.*)
CRYSTAL. What the hell? (*Lee goes over to the door, hooks on the chain.*)
LEE. Giant rats. Come on, I was just getting hot.
CRYSTAL. Somebody is out there.
LEE. Crystal, if you can't *use* it, lose it.
CRYSTAL. I taught you that one.
LEE. Freely admitted. Now . . .
LEE and CRYSTAL. (*Sing.*)
Ba doom, ba ba, ba ba, ba booom.

* See Special Note on copyright page.

44

Oh oh, uh, uh, ohhhhh

Heaven and . . .

(*The doorlock clicks open, and the door bangs against the chain.*)

MARK. (*From the hallway.*) Lee? Open the damn thing, willya? (*Lee unhooks the chain, and the door flies open. Mark, Eddie and Herman stumble in. Herman is barefoot, in his undershirt, but his pants are on. His hands are still tied behind him. Eddie has the package under his arm.*)

LEE. Jesus Christ.

MARK. You're telling me. (*Mark wrestles Herman to a sitting position on the couch.*)

LEE. It's the man next door.

HERMAN. You ladies must flee. These men are undesireables who will rape your tender parts and then—it's death.

CRYSTAL. Right on.

MARK. Crystal, don't encourage him.

CRYSTAL. What could this nut have said to you two big boys, that not only did you tie him up, but you brought him here?

HERMAN. Ching yuan bow li ting. Gwo shin!

MARK. (*To Herman.*) Come on, please. (*To Crystal and Lee.*) We were robbing him.

LEE. You what?

MARK. We were robbing him, and we blew it. He was there. He knew me.

LEE. You are kidding. I cannot believe this. *Robbing* him?

MARK. Dumb, hah?

LEE. And he walked in on you? Next door?

MARK. He didn't have to walk in. He was already there. What could we do?

LEE. You could've not done it, that's what. Eddie, how could you . . .

MARK. It wasn't Eddie.

LEE. Mark, couldn't you let me leave in peace, thinking everything would work out . . .

MARK. I just wanted to . . .

LEE. How could you be so stupid?

MARK. You mean to get caught?

LEE. No. You know what I mean.

CRYSTAL. Lee, you're screaming.

LEE. You noticed. Why the hell did you bring him here?

CRYSTAL. Cause the second they turn him loose he's gonna get the cops. Am I right, uh . . .

HERMAN. Herman. Yes.

EDDIE. Lee, we were only trying to . . .

LEE. I don't want to hear whatever crazy reason you two dreamed up to rob this poor bastard. More proof of your insanity I don't need. What I want to hear is what happens now.

EDDIE. *You* go to Sri Lanka in a few hours. *We* work it out.

LEE. Great. What exactly do you plan to do with him?

HERMAN. I am not him. I am me. My hands hurt. If you give me a drink of water, I will stop yelling. HELP! HELP! HELP! HELP! HELP! (*Herman keeps yelling. Crystal gets a large glass of water. She throws the drink in Herman's face. He is quiet. Then she feeds him what's left in the glass. He finishes it.*) Thank you. You know you can't sleep here. Only in the Port Authority. Show me your papers, all of you!

CRYSTAL. Herman, shut up. This is your problem too, believe me. (*Herman quiets.*) Good. (*To Mark and Eddie.*) You two are assholes. What did you steal?

MARK. Thirty dollars.

LEE. Beautiful.

EDDIE. And that. (*Eddie points to the package, which he's set down on the table.*)

LEE. Mark, I can listen now. Why did you do this?

MARK. Cause as of tomorrow the only company I'll have here is the roaches, and they'll be leaving soon, cause I'm gonna be stealing their food. Is that a reason?

LEE. Not really.

MARK. Rothman didn't tell me to hurry up on these fuckbooks today. He fired me. Me and Leisure Books are finished. How's that?

LEE. Why didn't you tell me?

MARK. It didn't seem like great going away news. You know, I want to talk about this like a reasonable four year old. I robbed this poor slob because. Because! Because! Shit! (*Mark slams his fist into the wall full force. He turns, starts ripping the endless sheets of paper out through the typewriters.*) You know this crap is an illustration of just what makes us humans so superior. Animals are in harmony with the universe! So what, I say! What animal would think to dress up like a nun and be whipped by a bald midget in

46

a Nazi uniform? None! Not even in the best zoos! Humans are still number one! (*The continuous sheets of paper fly everywhere, three long white banners, flapping and twisting. One of them lands on Herman, who begins to read avidly. Mark is threatening to wreck the place. Eddie grabs him from behind.*)

CRYSTAL. Mark, I see enough of this all day. Easy . . . easy . . . O.K.? (*Eddie lets Mark go.*)

HERMAN. (*Looking up from the sheet of typing he's been reading.*) Abner Dewitt! You are Abner Dewitt! I believe! (*Herman struggles up and over to Mark, the long sheet of typing in his teeth. Mark tears it out of his mouth.*) Autograph! You are a robber genius! (*Eddie pushes Herman back down on the couch. Mark tears the typescript Herman was reading into little pieces.*)

LEE. This is just beautiful. (*Crystal notices the package, where it has been knocked onto the floor in the scuffling. She picks it up.*)

CRYSTAL. Might as well. (*Crystal starts to open it, then stops to read the address. Reading:*) "To Miss Tracy Armison, 32 East 82nd St., New York. Fragile." (*She rips the package open. There is a note sitting on top of a mass of excelsior. Crystal has everyone's attention. She reads the note.*) "Dearest Twinkie, with all my love forever, John." (*Crystal digs into the packing. She removes a jewelry case. She opens it and takes out a necklace: a single large diamond drop on a gold chain.*) Uh oh. Pretty. You think it's real? (*Eddie comes over to her. He picks up the case, looks inside it.*)

EDDIE. Unless Tiffany's is selling rhinestones. (*Eddie takes the stone.*) Big looking mother, in a twenty-four carat setting. The thing's worth a few thousand at least.

CRYSTAL. You're kidding.

EDDIE. Un uh. Nothing to kid about. (*Mark comes over, takes the necklace out of Eddie's hand, walks toward Lee.*)

MARK. Try it on.

LEE. No thank you.

MARK. You might as well. It's yours.

LEE. I don't want it.

HERMAN. Mine! Yes!

EDDIE. Hey, Herman. You figured the package was worth something, didn't you? You were gonna rip off the delivery service!

HERMAN. *You* stole it. Beasts of the field, I name you: Eddie and Mark. Doors of the prison house gape wide for you. (*Her-*

man opens his mouth wide.) I am a slaughtered innocent. I was saving it for morning delivery.

EDDIE. Sure.

CRYSTAL. Maybe he's telling the truth.

MARK. Maybe, and maybe John spent his life savings to buy it for Twinkie, and maybe he's an honest man and made the money in a real estate deal, or a stock market deal, or a big movie deal. Or maybe John stole it. Or maybe he got it from the King of Siam, and who knows how the King got it. I'm one in a long line. (*Mark holds out the necklace to Lee. She takes it, puts it on. She looks in a mirror for a long moment. Mark draws her away from the mirror into his arms. He begins to dance with her. Herman is staring at them. Lee almost breaks away, but Mark holds on to her.*) Baby, I am a successful criminal mastermind . . . and I'm going with you. You heard what that necklace is worth. I'm going!

LEE. To Sri Lanka?

MARK. That's the place. We'll get a little house, you'll do your stuff, I'll write my book.

LEE. This is crazy, Mark. What if they catch you?

MARK. Catch *us*, my dear. Like Bonnie and Clyde. Belle Starr and Jesse James! Dr. Pepper and . . .

LEE. Mark, I . . .

MARK. They'll never find us. (*Lee takes off the necklace, puts it down on a table.*)

EDDIE. It's not so easy to sell something like that for what it's worth. I can do pretty good, I think. I'll send you the money.

CRYSTAL. Mr. Big.

EDDIE. I know a guy, that's all.

CRYSTAL. You know a guy. Wonderful. (*To Mark and Lee.*) So maybe you lovebirds can fly away. Meanwhile, back at the ranch, Herman goes to the cops and Mr. Big over there, necklace and all, is still around to hear the knock on his door.

MARK. I wasn't thinking.

CRYSTAL. Right again.

EDDIE. Nice to know you're looking out for me.

CRYSTAL. Nothing personal. (*Crystal goes to the counter, picks up a kitchen knife, walks toward Herman.*)

MARK. What the hell are you doing? (*Crystal cuts Herman's hands free.*)

CRYSTAL. Making sure he keeps his hands on his wrists. They were turning blue.

MARK. With hands, he's gonna run for the phone, or the door.

EDDIE. I'll watch him.

CRYSTAL. You do that. A space cadet like Herman could run for the window.

LEE. You think a saucer dropped him next door to keep an eye on us?

CRYSTAL. Maybe.

EDDIE. Maybe his little green friends are gonna come in and zap us with zeta rays.

CRYSTAL. Who gave you the right to make fun of me like that, you little crud? You think cause Lee can make fun of what I'm thinking, you're allowed? People that love me, they can make fun of me in my face. Not any schmuck off the street. Understand?

EDDIE. Hey, I was just talking. Every blonde bitch is the same. You think if you look good you can get away with every kind of shit.

LEE. Stop it, both of you. We're all going nuts enough here without Bill and Coo. (*Mark goes over to stand in front of Herman.*)

MARK. Lee, come over here. (*Lee joins him.*) Herman?

LEE. Mark, what are you doing?

MARK. I want him to see us. I want to tell him.

LEE. Tell him what?

MARK. Herman, I'm sorry about breaking into your place and all. It was crazy. I don't want to hurt you, or anyone. We just want to go away together. We love each other. Do you understand that?

HERMAN. I am a messenger for the Pony Express Messenger Service. Blessed are the meek like me. I hear both through the wall and I am not frightened sometimes at night as you are with me. I am in bed with you by hearing and mental seeing. Now you are both going away. The lady is going to travel, and the man is going to jail. The men will die like the Philistines, and be in Sing Sing. I was in bed with you, but no more. (*Herman jumps up as if to rush for the door. All four react, Mark and Eddie rushing to stop him. Herman stops himself, and grins at them.*) Murderers! Help! Boston Blackie! Bulldog Drummond! (*Herman sits, quite*

49

calmly. Mark puts his arm around Lee, comforting her.)

LEE. Mark, make this all be over, please. Can't we just go away from here . . .

MARK. Lee, it won't work. This is not the movies, where we hide out somewhere till the heat's off. He's seen all four of us, Eddie has a police record, and we don't know any defrocked doctors to give us all new faces.

HERMAN. Plastic faces are painful and do not move well. I read that in a magazine.

EDDIE. Thanks for the tip.

HERMAN. You are welcome. Four have a problem, which I am. We are five, with a problem. Otherwise you would not speak to me, and I know it to be true, as you have never done so in eight years of living with a wall between, though I say hello to both in the hall, and on the street as well. May I have another drink?

MARK. Help yourself. (*Herman mixes himself a bourbon and water. The four of them are silent, watching him. He takes a sip, puts the drink down.*)

HERMAN. Can I use the bathroom?

EDDIE. There a window in there?

LEE. No.

MARK. Go ahead. (*Herman exits into the bathroom, closes the door behind himself. The four talk softly.*)

EDDIE. I hate saying this, but maybe we could sort of have an accident or something.

MARK. You mean kill him?

EDDIE. I don't know. I figured someone ought to say it out loud.

MARK. Come on. What the hell game do you think this is? I was trying to find a few months rent without hurting anyone, and if a mouse had come up behind me I was ready to run. Now you're telling me we're gonna murder someone.

EDDIE. I didn't say that.

MARK. You came close.

EDDIE. Do you want to spend a few years in jail?

MARK. If that's the choice, yeah.

EDDIE. I thought you were going away with Lee. The new life!

LEE. Eddie, enough. You're as soft-hearted as he is.

EDDIE. So. At least I can see straight. I could get ten years. I'd be gray when I came out of there.

CRYSTAL. I'll play. Who's gonna kill him?

EDDIE. Who's taking his money? I could cover—torch his apartment. Leave the body inside, then burn the fucker. They'll figure a stove leak or something. Crystal and me are gone, and you two are flying high.

MARK. Eddie, that is so fucking horrible. You see him. How can you think that shit?

EDDIE. Look, Mark. I'm not the heavy in a book you're reading. I'm just trying to say something here. This is a bind, understand?

MARK. Yeah. Why don't you slit Herman's throat over the sink, and then ours to make sure we don't talk.

EDDIE. Hey, man . . .

MARK. You're an evil little bastard, aren't you. (*The toilet flushes. Herman comes out of the bathroom. He sits down quietly.*)

EDDIE. All right, maybe I'm an evil bastard, but I'm not a pussy. You're scared to live, and now your mommy is leaving and you're ready to cry. You're scared of working a fucking job to pay the rent cause maybe you won't be a fucking writer no more, whatever the hell you think that is. I ain't gonna wait for any fucking novel. If you know anything worth writing down to say to people, I'll hear it *right now*. (*Mark is silent.*) We got in a little trouble tonight, and instead of trying to get us out, you lay that candy-ass shit on me when I'm trying to help you. And me. You and me.

MARK. Eddie, listening to you about what to do is like getting directions from a drunk with a knife. I know you a long time. You were flunking out of high school, till your old man made you join the army. Then you screwed around at Fort Benning, till you got them to kick you out of the service. Back on the street, a few little scores, did a little time, and then you got a job driving a restaurant van, cause you had an Uncle. And then Uncle Leo hired this hippie chick as a waitress. Eileen. And you married her, gave her two kids in two years. She was nineteen, and she ran away from you and came back to those kids more times than I remember. Then Eileen got sick, and it was serious, so at last you did what she always wanted. You borrowed money

51

and moved to a little town in upstate New York, with trees and flowers, and an old station wagon. And then Eileen got sick again, and you went to church for the first time in fifteen years, and she died anyway. Then Eileen's mother came and took the kids away from you in court. You got your old job back, same lousy pay as before. You're alone. It's all turned to shit, Eddie. I know you still got your army forty-five in a drawer at home. Still keep it cause you're tough.. Why don't you go home and blow your brains out with it, instead of giving me advice? (*Eddie is shaken. He sits quietly. Herman leans toward him comfortingly.*)

HERMAN. Policemen will show you to the doctors . . .

CRYSTAL. Leave him alone! (*Crystal slaps Herman hard across the face. To Herman:*) You got these two blind men pissing on each other, and you led 'em there and told 'em it's the toilet. I hope you keep wandering around and around in your head. One day you're gonna step behind a tree in there and disappear for good.

LEE. Crys . . .

CRYSTAL. What do you want, Lee? You think I should lay off him cause he's crazy or something? If he's really nuts, down deep, it won't matter. If he's not, let him hear. (*Crystal sits down.*)

MARK. Eddie, I'm sorry, I didn't mean to . . .

EDDIE. Me neither. It's O.K. (*In the silence, Herman starts sobbing.*)

CRYSTAL. Oh, Jesus. (*Herman stops himself.*)

HERMAN. I hear you all, and for your feelings that burn me inside, I make today your birthday. I give a gift to you. I have an erection now from fear and love. It is for all four of you, and secret. I give you the necklace. I stole it for me. My lie for me is ready. I am bonded and believed. (*Herman points to the cut on his forehead.*) By reason of my wound, the package was taken from me on the street. I will tell my lie for you. (*Herman presses his forefinger against his lips in the gesture of silence.*) I am forgetting you. You can go, and become strong with money, and fly. (*Everyone is quiet. Suddenly Mark leaps up, goes over to Herman and hugs him.*)

MARK. Hey . . . thank you. Thank you. I don't know what to say. Hey! Lee! I'm going! I'm coming! I mean I'm gonna be there in the air. Up, up and away! I gotta pack. I gotta . . .

EDDIE. Mark, hold on. I don't believe him. He's scared. He's listened to every word we've said in here. You think he loves us now? You think he doesn't know where you're going? You think Sri Lanka is out of this world, and they ain't got an American Consulate and they can't find you?

That hunk of jewelry is his. First thief. He'll never get another shot. If he tells his dumb story they probably won't arrest him, but he'll get fired for sure. He'll never work another messenger job. What's he gonna do? He's gonna end up in the Men's Shelter. You think he doesn't know that? He knows how to dial. If he's not telling the truth, you two won't even get to the airport.

LEE. And there's you.

EDDIE. I want to believe him as much as you do, Lee, but I can't put ten years of my goddamn life on his word. He's changed his feelings too fast, and he's got too much to lose.

HERMAN. NO! I AM TRUE! I FORGIVE EVERYONE! (*Herman again makes the sign of silence, forefinger on lips.*)

EDDIE. Bullshit.

LEE. I believe him.

MARK. Lee, use your head. Why would he . . .

LEE. Don't ask me why, Mark. I don't know. (*Silence for a long moment.*)

MARK. Herman, you got a mother living? Father? Kids? Any relatives? (*Herman is silent to each question. He finally speaks.*)

HERMAN. You four. And then none.

LEE. What are you asking, Mark? Anyone with no one to miss him, no one depending on him, and no one to come looking for him, step behind this little door.

MARK. I am just asking.

LEE. Sure. Now the both of you are fucking crazy.

CRYSTAL. Lee, *calm down.*

LEE. The hell I will. I got a little job somewhere, so everybody got themselves into this. Now, I'll get you out of it, and you can all go the hell home. (*Lee picks up the kitchen knife off the table. She rushes at Herman with it. Herman screams in terror. Mark grabs her, wraps his arms around her.*)

MARK. Are you nuts?

LEE. Yes! Let me go! (*To Eddie and Crystal.*) You two dump him in an alley somewhere. Gimme the damn necklace! I'll sell it on the street! (*Mark twists the knife out of Lee's hand. It falls to the floor. She is sobbing.*) Mark, I want to leave now. Let's go to the airplane. Please. (*Lee is pulling him toward the door. Mark finally stops her.*)

MARK. Lee, we can't. It's too big a chance. (*Eddie picks up the knife. He takes one step toward Herman, who stares at him, frozen with fear.*)

EDDIE. Just kidding. (*He tosses the knife in a corner.*)

CRYSTAL. That's it. Great bunch of killers. Herman, my boy, they'll send you drop dead postcards from jail. You just do whatever the hell you'll do. And so will we. (*Herman is coming out of his daze of terror. His face is twitching. One arm seems out of control. It swings aimlessly. He stands, looks at Lee.*)

HERMAN. You are a lady, and I never hurt you. I would have lied to the policemen for you. I would have gone to a bad place for you. Then I saw my blood on the knife. I am becoming sick. You all want the world for you and have no mercy on other life, such as yours truly. You do not love me. You kill me like a sheep. I am a human being of the first kind. My imagination is a cancer, but I am healing myself. I can communicate without wires and without dixiecups. I told Jesus I would not go to his church but my own and he kissed me. I am the purple flower of this city, and you are my food and my shit, all four of you. The ladies special.

(*To Lee.*) For you, Sri Lanka will be hell. Your plane will crash into a lake of fire, and you will burn forever, and you will be raped by sharks, and bleed into the sea. (*Herman advances toward Lee, as if to strangle or embrace her.*) Bitch. Bleed for me. Bleed for the messenger. (*Mark steps between them. Herman won't stop. Mark punches him in the belly. He hits him again, his fist driving into Herman's chest. Herman crumples to the floor. He begins to twitch spasmodically. Mark steps back, frightened, not understanding. They stare. Herman begins to spasm, going into convulsions, his whole body wrenching back and forth in a contorted parody of sex, or a horrific speeded up rigor mortis. It is an epileptic fit. He flops about like a fish on the dock. Crystal, a nurse, is the first to understand what Mark's beating has triggered. She goes to Herman, kneels by him. He grabs her hands in his in a powerful grip.*)

CRYSTAL. Get me something to put between his teeth! Eddie, help me! Don't restrain him! (*Eddie grabs a rag, hands it to Crystal. Herman's convulsions are still violent, and he hangs desperately onto*

Crystal, who is trying to get the rag between his teeth so he won't bite or swallow his tongue.) Eddie! Get his mouth open! Get it in!

EDDIE. Got it! (*Crystal and Eddie have gotten a portion of the rag into Herman's mouth, and something under his head.*)

CRYSTAL. Okay. (*Quieter.*) Okay. (*Herman quiets somewhat, still hanging on to Crystal's hands, his body still twitching.*) He's gotta have some medication. Dilantin, or phenobarb, or . . .

MARK. Eddie, the pills. (*Eddie remembers, digs the pills out of his pocket, hands them to Crystal. Crystal looks at the label.*)

CRYSTAL. He's an epileptic on a heavy dose. Anti-convulsants. That scene just set him off. It happens. Keep back and let him rest. (*Crystal takes the rag out of Herman's mouth, then covers him with a blanket. She takes Herman's pulse. First light of dawn at the window. Silence as Crystal times Herman's heartbeat. She's done. Herman is quiet. Crystal nods. The other three relax slightly. Crystal remains over Herman.*) He's O.K. He's gonna be O.K. It's gone now. He'll sleep for awhile. We'll give him a pill when he wakes up.

MARK. (*To Lee.*) I don't know what happened, babe. He was cursing you. I just . . .

LEE. Mark, it's all right. You didn't know.

MARK. Crys, he's gonna be O.K., hah?

CRYSTAL. I told you, he'll be all right. He's gotta rest. (*Crystal looks at her watch.*) You two don't have much time. You've got a plane to catch.

MARK. Nothing's settled. We can't. . . .

EDDIE. Nothing's gonna be settled. Lee's advance money'll get you on the plane. I got the damn necklace. I'll get what I can for it, and send it to you. Till then, live cheap. You got practice. (*Eddie picks the necklace up off the table, stuffs it in his pocket.*) And I'll sort things out with Herman. We'll give him some of the money or something.

MARK. Eddie, he's crazy.

CRYSTAL. He's not crazy.

EDDIE. Look, Marko, this time is over for you and Lee. This place is over. Now you wash your hands, pick up your check, take your hat off the rack, and go. Understand? I'll take care of it.

CRYSTAL. Lee, tell him. Go. You got an hour. You can still get to the airport on time.

MARK. What am I gonna do in Sri Lanka?

CRYSTAL. You were telling us.

MARK. That was years ago.

LEE. You are gonna eat mangoes, drink palm wine, love me all night and sit in dirty cafes by the beach all day, writing about New York.

EDDIE. Get outta here. Crystal and me will nurse the baby, and then deal with him.

MARK. I'm not packed or anything.

LEE. They might have clothes in Sri Lanka. If not, you can go naked for a few weeks till we make some out of leaves.

EDDIE. Time! The way out is through the door. A clever couple like you two can't seem to find it.

MARK. Here goes nothing. (*To Lee.*) Love me?

LEE. Just what I was about to ask you.

CRYSTAL. Would you two shut up and get out of here. (*Crystal hugs them both. So does Eddie. Mark and Lee pick up Lee's suitcases, head for the door.*)

LEE. Crys, here's the keys to this place. Give them to the landlord, or throw them away.

CRYSTAL. Sure. (*Mark and Lee go out the door. Crystal shuts it behind them. First rays of sunlight through the window. Eddie sits and begins to sing to himself.*)

EDDIE. (*Sings.*)

Earth Angel, earth angel, will you be miiine

My darling dear, love you all the tiiime . . .*

(*Crystal goes to the window, looks down onto the street. She turns back to the room.*)

CRYSTAL. They got a cab.

EDDIE. (*Sings.*)

I'm just a foooool . . .

CRYSTAL. Hey, they got a cab.

EDDIE. How's Herman? (*Crystal does not need to look. She knows.*)

CRYSTAL. He's dead.

EDDIE. (*Sings.*)

I'm just a foooool, a fool in love . . .

CRYSTAL. He's dead.

EDDIE. I heard you. That's what I figured.

CRYSTAL. We better call an ambulance.

EDDIE. What for? Trouble? (*Eddie looks over at Herman's body.*)

*Used by permission of Dootsie Williams Publications.

I'll put him in his own bed, in a minute. Hey, buddy, don't you want to die at home? (*Eddie lights a cigarette.*) Jesus, I'm tired.

CRYSTAL. Me, too. (*Crystal gets up, puts on her coat.*) I need to get some sleep. I'm going home. (*Crystal looks over at Eddie, takes a step toward the door.*) You wanna walk me? (*They freeze. Lights fade to black. As houselights come up, the Del-Vikings "Come Go With Me" over house speakers.*)*

Love love you darling, come and go with me
Please don't send me, way beyond the sea
I love you darling, so come go with me

Come come come come, come into my heart
Tell me darling, we will never part
I need you darling, so come go with me

Come on go with me
Come on go with me
Come on go with me

END OF PLAY

PROPERTY LIST

Anthropological artifacts (Hopi Kachina doll, Indonesian mask,
    etc.)
Bed
Blood
Book
Bookcases (made of orange crates)
Book rack with National Geographics
Bouquet of flowers
Bottle of Jack Daniels
Bottle of pills
Bottles of beer
Cassette tape recorder
Cassette tapes
Chairs
Cigarettes
Cocktail table
Coffee cans
Couch
Crumpled piece of paper (in Herman's pocket)
Desk (made out of old door)
Diamond necklace
Dresser (in Herman's apartment)
Drying rack with sox
Flashlight
Glasses
Groceries (celery, carrots, zucchini, etc.)
Ice tray
Jewelry case
Key
Kitchen knife
Kitchen sinks
Lamp (in Herman's apartment)
Maps of continents
Money/change
Manuscript
Napkin
Package (small)
Picture of Jesus (on wall)

Playboy centerfold (on wall)
Porno novels
Posters
Purse
Rag
Refrigerator
Rock
Rolling stool
Rope
Scattered clothes (on Herman's floor)
Screwdriver
Serving tray
Shopping bag
Stack of money
Suitcase (battered)
Suitcases (2 — Lee's)
Table
Telephone
Tiffany box
Typewriters (3 — with rolls of paper)
Watches (Herman and Lee)

PRODUCTION NOTE

The set for FIVE OF US requires two adjoining apartment areas, and an area or areas that can be used for street, hallway, and the bar scene. Herman's apartment is predominantly his bedroom, while Mark and Lee's is predominantly their living room, and a bathroom. The main area should be Mark and Lee's apartment, where almost all of Act II takes place. There should be some indication in the design that these are apartments that share a wall in the same building, though this wall need not be literal, and the apartments can blend into each other, and be defined by floor pattern, furniture, and lighting.

MUSIC NOTE

The early rock and roll songs used in this text of FIVE OF US are:* "Earth Angel" — The Penguins; "Stay" — Maurice Williams and the Zodiacs; "Whole Lotta Fish In the Sea" — Marvellettes; "Blanche" — Three Friends; "Heaven and Paradise" — Don Julian and the Meadowlarks; "Come Go With Me" — Del Vikings. These songs may certainly be changed for others in a particular production, choosing other rock material with a similar "dated" feel. Any group licensed to perform FIVE OF US who wish to include the song STAY in their presentation of the play must secure prior written permission from: CHERIO CORP., 39 W. 54th St., N.Y., N.Y. 10019.

COME GO WITH ME is not authorized for performance unless express permission will have been granted in each case by GIL MUSIC CORP., 1650 Broadway, N.Y., N.Y. 10019.

* See Special Note on copyright page.

NEW PLAYS

• **A QUESTION OF MERCY by David Rabe.** The Obie Award-winning playwright probes the sensitive and controversial issue of doctor-assisted suicide in the age of AIDS in this poignant drama. *"There are many devastating ironies in Mr. Rabe's beautifully considered, piercingly clear-eyed work ... " –The NY Times. "With unsettling candor and disturbing insight, the play arouses pity and understanding of a troubling subject ... Rabe's provocative tale is an affirmation of dignity that rings clear and true."* –Variety. [6M, 1W] ISBN: 0-8222-1643-4

• **A DOLL'S HOUSE by Henrik Ibsen, adapted by Frank McGuinness. Winner of the 1997 Tony Award for best revival.** *"New, raw, gut-twisting and gripping. Easily the hottest drama this season."* –USA Today. *"Bold, brilliant and alive."* –The Wall Street Journal. *"A thunderclap of an evening that takes your breath away."* –Time. *"The stuff of Broadway legend."* –Associated Press. [4M, 4W, 2 boys] ISBN: 0-8222-1636-1

• **THE WAITING ROOM by Lisa Loomer.** Three women from different centuries meet in a doctor's waiting room in this dark comedy about the timeless quest for beauty -- and its cost. *" ... THE WAITING ROOM ... is a bold, risky melange of conflicting elements that is ... terrifically moving ... There's no resisting the fierce emotional pull of the play."* – The NY Times. *" ... one of the high points of this year's Off-Broadway season ... THE WAITING ROOM is well worth a visit."* –Back Stage. [7M, 4W, flexible casting] ISBN: 0-8222-1594-2

• **MR. PETERS' CONNECTIONS by Arthur Miller.** Mr. Miller describes the protagonist as existing in a dream-like state when the mind is "freed to roam from real memories to conjectures, from trivialities to tragic insights, from terror of death to glorying in one's being alive." With this memory play, the Tony Award and Pulitzer Prize-winner reaffirms his stature as the world's foremost dramatist. *" ... a cross between Joycean stream-of-consciousness and Strindberg's dream plays, sweetened with a dose of William Saroyan's philosophical whimsy ... CONNECTIONS is most intriguing ... Miller scholars will surely find many connections of their own to make between this work and the author's earlier plays."* –The NY Times. [5M, 3W] ISBN: 0-8222-1687-6

• **THE STEWARD OF CHRISTENDOM by Sebastian Barry.** A freely imagined portrait of the author's great-grandfather, the last Chief Superintendent of the Dublin Metropolitan Police. *"MAGNIFICENT ... the cool, elegiac eye of James Joyce's THE DEAD; the bleak absurdity of Samuel Beckett's lost, primal characters; the cosmic anger of KING LEAR ..."* –The NY Times. *"Sebastian Barry's compassionate imaging of an ancestor he never knew is among the most poignant onstage displays of humanity in recent memory."* –Variety. [5M, 4W] ISBN: 0-8222-1609-4

• **SYMPATHETIC MAGIC by Lanford Wilson. Winner of the 1997 Obie for best play.** The mysteries of the universe, and of human and artistic creation, are explored in this award-winning play. *"Lanford Wilson's idiosyncratic SYMPATHETIC MAGIC is his BEST PLAY YET ... the rare play you WANT ... chock-full of ideas, incidents, witty or poetic lines, scientific and philosophical argument ... you'll find your intellectual faculties racing."* – New York Magazine. *"The script is like a fully notated score, next to which most new plays are cursory lead sheets."* –The Village Voice. [5M, 3W] ISBN: 0-8222-1630-2

DRAMATISTS PLAY SERVICE, INC.
440 Park Avenue South, New York, NY 10016 212-683-8960 Fax 212-213-1539
postmaster@dramatists.com www.dramatists.com

NEW PLAYS

• SMASH by Jeffrey Hatcher. Based on the novel, AN UNSOCIAL SOCIALIST by George Bernard Shaw, the story centers on a millionaire Socialist who leaves his bride on their wedding day because he fears his passion for her will get in the way of his plans to overthrow the British government. *"SMASH is witty, cunning, intelligent, and skillful."* –Seattle Weekly. *"SMASH is a wonderfully high-style British comedy of manners that evokes the world of Shaw's high-minded heroes and heroines, but shaped by a post modern sensibility."* –Seattle Herald. [5M, 5W] ISBN: 0-8222-1553-5

• PRIVATE EYES by Steven Dietz. A comedy of suspicion in which nothing is ever quite what it seems. *"Steven Dietz's ... Pirandellian smooch to the mercurial nature of theatrical illusion and romantic truth, Dietz's spiraling structure and breathless pacing provide enough of an oxygen rush to revive any moribund audience member ... Dietz's mastery of playmaking ... is cause for kudos."* –The Village Voice. *"The cleverest and most artful piece presented at the 21st annual [Humana] festival was PRIVATE EYES by writer-director Steven Dietz."* –The Chicago Tribune. [3M, 2W] ISBN: 0-8222-1619-1

• DIMLY PERCEIVED THREATS TO THE SYSTEM by Jon Klein. Reality and fantasy overlap with hilarious results as this unforgettable family attempts to survive the nineties. *"Here's a play whose point about fractured families goes to the heart, mind -- and ears."* –The Washington Post. *" ... an end-of-the millennium comedy about a family on the verge of a nervous breakdown ... Trenchant and hilarious ... "* –The Baltimore Sun. [2M, 4W] ISBN: 0-8222-1677-9

• HONOUR by Joanna Murray-Smith. In a series of intense confrontations, a wife, husband, lover and daughter negotiate the forces of passion, lust, history, responsibility and honour. *"Tight, crackling dialogue (usually played out in punchy verbal duels) captures characters unable to deal with emotions ... Murray-Smith effectively places her characters in situations that strip away pretense."* –Variety. *"HONOUR might just capture a few honors of its own."* –Time Out Magazine. [1M, 3W] ISBN: 0-8222-1683-3

• NINE ARMENIANS by Leslie Ayvazian. A revealing portrait of three generations of an Armenian-American family. *" ... Ayvazian's obvious personal exploration ... is evocative, and her picture of an American Life colored nostalgically by an increasingly alien ethnic tradition, is persuasively embedded into a script of a certain supple grace ... "* –The NY Post. *"... NINE ARMENIANS is a warm, likable work that benefits from ... Ayvazian's clear-headed insight into the dynamics of a close-knit family ... "* –Variety. [5M, 5W] ISBN: 0-8222-1602-7

• PSYCHOPATHIA SEXUALIS by John Patrick Shanley. Fetishes and psychiatry abound in this scathing comedy about a man and his father's argyle socks. *"John Patrick Shanley's new play, PSYCHOPATHIA SEXUALIS is ... perfectly poised between daffy comedy and believable human neurosis which Shanley combines so well ... "* –The LA Times. *"John Patrick Shanley's PSYCHOPATHIA SEXUALIS is a salty boulevard comedy with a bittersweet theme ... "* –New York Magazine. *"A tour de force of witty, barbed dialogue."* –Variety. [3M, 2W] ISBN: 0-8222-1615-9

DRAMATISTS PLAY SERVICE, INC.
440 Park Avenue South, New York, NY 10016 212-683-8960 Fax 212-213-1539
postmaster@dramatists.com www.dramatists.com